The Hidden Cost of Poor Mobile App Performance

Parekh

Contents

1 Introduction   1

  1.1 Mobile Subscribers, Data Usage, and Churn in United States and Canada 1

    1.1.1 Customer Churn 2

  1.2 Customer Satisfaction, Loyalty, and Retention 2

  1.3 Quality of Service 3

  1.4 Quality of Experience 4

  1.5 Relationship between QoS and QoE 4

  1.6 Problem Statement 5

  1.7 book Scope 6

  1.8 book Outline 6

2 Background Information   7

  2.1 Measuring Quality of Service 7

    2.1.1 Drive Testing 7

      2.1.1.1 Disadvantages of Drive Testing 8

    2.1.2 Crowdsourced Network Data 9

| | | 2.1.2.1 | Benefits of Crowdsourced Network Data | 9 |

2.1.2.1   Benefits of Crowdsourced Network Data 9

2.1.2.2   Minimization of Drive Test 9

2.1.2.3   Smartphone-based Applications 10

2.1.2.4   Open Source Tools 10

2.2   Factors Affecting QoS 10

     2.2.1   Estimating User Density to Improve End-User Experience . . 11

         2.2.1.1   Population Distribution 11

     2.2.2   Usage Patterns of Mobile Subscribers 12

         2.2.2.1   Mobile Application Usage 13

     2.2.3   Placement of Cell Towers and Wireless Access Points 13

     2.2.4   Network Performance Tuning 13

2.3   Chapter Summary 14

3   Description Of Mobile Network Data And Pre-Processing Steps   15

3.1   Data Collection 17

     3.1.1   Location, QoS Parameters, and Timestamp 17

     3.1.2   Database Query 21

3.2   Data Pre-processing 25

     3.2.1   Data Standardization 25

     3.2.2   Data Validation 27

     3.2.3   Data Mapping and Conversion 27

3.3   Verification of Pre-Processed Data 28

3.4   Data Pipeline 30

3.5   Chapter Summary 32

4   Mobile Subscriber Density in a Network   33

4.1   Kernel Density Estimation 33

4.2   Expectation Maximization 36

4.3   EM and KDE Validation 40

4.4   Selection of KDE Kernels 44

4.5   Numerical Instability and Data Scaling 49

4.6   Chapter Summary 55

5   Analysis of User Density and Quality of Service   56

5.1   Statistical Analysis of User Distribution 56

     5.1.1   Anderson-Darling Test Procedure 57

	5.1.2	Anderson-Darling Test Implementation and Validation	59
	5.1.3	Anderson-Darling Test Results	65
5.2	User Density Distribution		69
5.3	Quality of Service Analysis of Mobile Users		78
	5.3.1	Comparison of QoS Parameters	81

5.1.2 Anderson-Darling Test Implementation and Validation 59
5.1.3 Anderson-Darling Test Results 65
5.2 User Density Distribution 69
5.3 Quality of Service Analysis of Mobile Users 78
5.3.1 Comparison of QoS Parameters 81
5.3.1.1 Download Throughput 81
5.3.1.2 Upload Throughput 86
5.3.1.3 Latency Average 90
5.3.1.4 Jitter Average 94
5.3.1.5 Signal Strength 97
5.3.1.6 Insights from QoS Analysis 100
5.4 Chapter Summary 101

6 Conclusions 102
6.1 Results 102
6.2 Further Analyses 103

A Additional Information 104
A.1 Great Circle Distance Query 104
A.2 Estimated PDF of Mobile Network Data 105

Chapter 1

Introduction

Rapid progress in wireless communications technologies has allowed mobile users to use applications such as VoIP, real-time video streaming, gaming, social media, and much more. The richness of mobile device applications means that users now experience the quality of service (QoS) of a wireless network via the applications they use. Quality of service is the collective effect of service performance which determines the degree of satisfaction of a user of the service [78]. As mobile applications such as real-time video streaming place a high demand on the network QoS, inadequate user-perceived QoS levels can cause users to switch their network service provider.

In service industries, such as telecommunications, the cost of acquiring a new customer is substantially higher than the cost of retaining a present customer [42] [79]. Also, the long-term relationship between a customer and its telecommunications network operator is of great importance in determining the company's success within competitive markets [43]. Therefore, customer retention and avoiding customer churn are of critical importance to telecommunication companies, with poor user-perceived QoS being one of the significant sources of customer churn.

1.1 Mobile Subscribers, Data Usage, and Churn in United States and Canada

According to the Numbering Resource Utilization Forecast (NRUF) and Cellular Telecommunications and Internet Association (CTIA), there were approximately 398 million mobile wireless subscriber connections at the end of 2016 in United States, with 261.9 million being smartphone connections [31]. Also, CTIA reported monthly data usage per smartphone subscriber at 3.9 GB per month from 2015-2016 [31]. Furthermore, total wireless service revenues in United States were reported to be approximately \$189 billion [31].

On the other hand, the number of mobile subscribers in Canada reached 33.3 million in 2018, with 81% of Canadians, 18 years or older, owning a smartphone [76]. Mobile wireless has been the fastest-growing telecommunications sector in Canada making a revenue of \$27.1 billion in 2018 [76]. Also, revenues from mobile data services were one of the main drivers for this strong revenue growth, with an estimated \$10.9 billion. The use of smartphones and tablets increased the volume of network data traffic, and average data usage was 2 GB per month per mobile data subscriber in 2017 [76]. Data usage included the use of data for video streaming services such as Netflix and YouTube, as well as audio streaming services such as Spotify [76]. In 2018, data usage (GB/h) over a wireless LTE network was reported to be: 0.14 for Spotify, 0.32 for Netflix, 0.60 for YouTube, 1.43 for CBC TV, and 1.90 for CraveTV [76]. With an increase in mobile data usage, specifically for streaming video content, there has been an increase in revenue for AVOD services (advertising video-on-demand services such as YouTube). In 2018, AVOD services generated 59% of their revenue from mobile platforms, with the total revenue being \$1.3 billion [76].

1.1.1 Customer Churn

Customer churn is described as the process of subscribers switching from one service provider to another [19]. It is calculated by dividing the aggregate number of wireless subscriber connections who canceled service during a time period by the total number of wireless subscriber connections at the beginning of that time period. The average monthly churn rate for Canadian wireless carriers from 2014 to 2018 was from 1.56% to 1.44 [76]. In the United States, the average monthly churn rate from the first quarter of 2013 to the fourth quarter of 2016 was from 1.42% to 1.85% [31].

1.2 Customer Satisfaction, Loyalty, and Retention

Customer retention is shown to be linked with customer satisfaction and customer loyalty, which in turn are related to a customer's perceived quality of service [13] [100] [21]. Anderson and Sullivan [13] found that when perceived product quality falls short of expectations, it has a greater impact on satisfaction and repurchase intentions than quality which exceeds expectations.

Bolton conducted a 22-month study in the cellular telephone industry focusing on customers' perception and behavior [21]. The author of [21] concluded that customers form expectations about the value of the service based on their prior cumulative satisfaction and that these expectations change depending on new experiences, such as service transactions or failures. Also, Gerpott et al. [43] surveyed 684 cellular network customers in Germany and found that customer satisfaction has a significant impact on customer loyalty, which in turn influences a customer's decision to terminate/extend a contractual relationship with their wireless service provider. Furthermore, Ahn, Lee, and Han [10] sampled 10,000 customers in the telecommunications service industry in South Korea and determined that service quality, such as call drop or connection failure, is directly related to customer retention.

Jones and Sasser [48] mentioned that complete customer satisfaction is the key to securing customer loyalty and generating superior long-term financial performance. The authors of [48] argued that in a highly competitive market, there is a tremendous difference between the loyalty of *merely* satisfied and *completely* satisfied customers, with only *completely* satisfied customers exhibiting loyalty.

The wireless telecommunications sector is a highly competitive market, and customer satisfaction is one of the contributing factors of industry churn [31] [76]. For a network servicer provider, delivering a high level of QoS to customers to improve their experience with mobile applications can help guarantee long-term customer retention and financial gain.

1.3   Quality of Service

Within the service quality literature, quality focuses on meeting customer needs and requirements [66]. It is a measure of how well the service level delivered matches customers' expectations [60].

In the telecommunications literature, quality of service is a set of specific requirements provided by a network to users, which are necessary to achieve the required functionality of an application or a service [33]. QoS parameters are a quantitative measure such as jitter, delay, packet loss, bandwidth, and throughput.

There is an asymmetry between network-side QoS perceptions and the mobile device-side QoS level experienced by users. This difference arises as the network is unaware of the apps a user is interacting with and the service demand each given user may be expecting a wireless network to provide at any given time.

1.4 Quality of Experience

Smartphone users perceive QoS more subjectively, and this subjective perception of the users is called Quality of Experience (QoE) [87]. Low QoS support on the network-side can affect a user's experience with mobile apps; however, QoS measurements such as delay or packet loss do not fully capture the user-perceived quality of the network. Mean Opinion Score (MOS) is a common way to assess user perception of network-level performance. But given the multitude of applications on the Internet today, conducting experiments in a controlled environment with new traffic characteristics and performance requirements is too expensive [87]. Also, MOS values are prone to misuse or misinterpretation and are highly influenced by the choices made in the experiment design [90].

To capture users' perceptions when using a network application, Chen et al. presented a framework called OneClick, which allowed users to click a dedicated key when dissatisfied with the quality of an app [25]. Joumblatt et al. [49] used machine learning models to build predictors of user dissatisfaction. Also, Aggarwal et al. implemented an approach called Prometheus to estimate QoE metrics of applications by monitoring the app's network traffic [9]. Furthermore, Dimoupoulos et al. developed a methodology for detecting video streaming QoE issues from encrypted traffic [36].

1.5 Relationship between QoS and QoE

QoE defines the overall performance of a network from the user perspective, whereas QoS focuses on quantitative network-side measurements such as jitter, packet loss, delay, etc. To avoid customer churn, knowing about user experiences and perceptions of the overall network quality can be useful to the network service providers. QoS metrics do not directly capture a user's interaction with a mobile application, but numerous studies have attempted to explain the relationship between QoS and QoE. Khirman et al. defined a non-linear relationship between QoS and QoE and found that network bandwidth plays a crucial role in end-user satisfaction [53]. Fiedler et al. derived an exponential relationship between QoS and QoE called IQX hypothesis and assessed streaming services by expressing Mean Opinion Score (i.e., QoE) as a function of loss and jitter [40]. Shaikh et al. investigated correlations between user-perceived QoE and QoS by using users' Mean Opinion Scores and network-side parameters such as loss ratio, download times, and throughput [87]. Katsarakis et al. used a feature selection algorithm to build optimal QoE predictors using features from network QoS metrics [52]. Sermpezis et al. built statistical models to predict user experience as a function of QoS and proposed a recommendation system for QoS-aware multimedia services [84].

1.6 Problem Statement

The challenge of providing QoS support for wireless networks is an open research problem. QoS schemes such as load balancing [30] [18] [98] [16], admission control [95] [74] [46] [64] [11], link adaptation [28] [15] [91] and scheduling [14] [62] [58] have been implemented for different network layers.

However, users of mobile applications are generally unaware of network-side QoS management as they experience the network quality through their apps. If the users find the experience to be unsatisfactory, then there is a possibility that he/she may switch the network service provider [57] [69] [72].

As the density of users connected to a wireless network increases, QoS of the network can start to decrease. This effect is more observable in a highly dense urban area, where the population is dynamic. When people move about within the city, the density can change from morning to evening or from one week to the next. As groups of people commute to work or conduct various activities, they stay connected on their mobile devices and access wireless Internet. A high volume of users accessing the wireless network at the same time can cause the network-side QoS levels to degrade, thereby affecting the experience of the users with their mobile apps.

The goal of this **book** is to directly assess via data: i) how user densities change in an urban environment and, ii) how these changes impact device-side QoS measurements.

1.7 book Scope

This book has the following goals:

1. To analyze changes in user density over time using mobile network data from a densely populated region such as Manhattan. Based on the location information associated with device-side QoS measurments, the distribution of users throughout the region is estimated as a probability density function.

2. To study the impact of user density on network QoS by evaluating QoS parameters of high, medium, and low density areas. QoS parameters, as contained in the data, are device-side measurements such as packet loss, jitter, throughput, etc. The device-side measurements describe the state of the wireless network from the users' perspective.

1.8 book Outline

This book is organized as follows:

Chapter 1 states the main research goal and describes the problem, its impact, and the overall structure of this document.

Chapter 2 provides background information on the drive testing method and its disadvantages, presents the benefits of using crowdsourced data to analyze network performance, and discusses factors affecting the end-user quality of service in a cellular mobile network.

Chapter 3 describes the mobile network data and explains the data pre-processing and verification steps.

Chapter 4 explains the algorithms such as Kernel Density Estimation and Expectation Maximization to estimate the user density distribution.

Chapter 5 discusses the statistical analysis of user density estimates using the k-sample Anderson-Darling test and compares the users' QoS levels for high, medium, and low density areas.

Chapter 6 restates the problem, summarizes results and analysis, and concludes the new solution and its contribution.

Chapter 2

Background Information

Each new generation of mobile network technology brings a new set of expectations for mobile users allowing network service providers to attract and retain customers. As more features become available through mobile technology, users expect to have network service available anytime, anywhere. However, with each leap into the next generation of wireless network technology such as 3G, 4G, LTE, and 5G, there exist new and more complex QoS challenges. Also, emerging areas such as Smart Cities, autonomous vehicles, Internet of Things (IOT), etc. are expected to place further demands on wireless network QoS.

2.1 Measuring Quality of Service

QoS measurements provide the network service provider with information about the state of the network. Drive testing and crowdsourced data are the most common methods used by network service providers to assess network performance at the end-user level.

2.1.1 Drive Testing

Drive testing is a method of measuring and assessing the coverage, capacity, and QoS of a mobile network [22]. The technique consists of driving a motor vehicle containing specialized equipment that can detect and record a wide variety of cellular service parameters in a given geographical area [22]. By measuring what a wireless network subscriber would experience in any specific area, wireless carriers can make directed changes to their networks to provide better coverage and service to their customers [22].

Weissberger et al. assessed QoS of the UMTS network for background services such as e-mail and text messaging in the United States [93]. The authors [93] collected data through drive test measurements, calculated QoS parameters, and derived data quality index to indicate network performance as experienced by the users. Also, Kostanic et al. evaluated the QoS performance of three major cellular voice and data networks in the US through drive test measurements [55]. The authors used performance indicators, as viewed as important from a user's perspective, to compare QoS between cellular networks with different access technologies [55]. Furthermore, Kadioglu et al. assessed QoS of major cellular networks in Turkey by measuring key performance indicators (KPIs) using the drive test method [50]. The authors [50] used KPIs based on user perspective about network performance and compared the speech quality of different wireless carriers. Moreover, Rufini et al. analyzed the QoS performance of Italian mobile network operators using drive-test measurements to inform users about the network performance achieved in different areas [82].

Currently, companies such as Rohde & Schwarz [6], GL communications Inc. [4], Nielson [5], and Applus+ [1] provide a variety of drive test solutions for wireless carriers to enable them to assess, optimize, benchmark, and troubleshoot network performance.

2.1.1.1 Disadvantages of Drive Testing

The traditional method of drive testing has the following drawbacks:

1. Conducting drive tests is expensive and time consuming while requiring significant human effort.

2. Detailed network measurements may only cover small areas within the network as covering an entire city is expensive.

3. Drive testing provides snapshots of a network's operation generally separated by months in time. Drive testing does not provide continual daily assessments of network QoS.

2.1.2 Crowdsourced Network Data

Crowdsourcing is an alternative method of assessing the performance of a wireless network by using users' equipments (UEs) in the network to automatically collect measurement data [38]. Many carriers have rolled out smart applications, firmware, and standardization efforts to crowdsource network data with the help of UEs [38]. With crowdsourcing, the QoS measurements are more reflective of the real-time network quality as they represent a sample of users' devices that actively record QoS levels as they move through and use the network.

2.1.2.1 Benefits of Crowdsourced Network Data

The following are the benefits of using crowdsourced data to analyze network performance:

1. It is cost-effective and can cover a large geographical area.

2. It can easily adapt to new mobile device usage modes and new mobile apps.

3. Large amounts of data can be collected in a short period of time [39].

4. Network performance metrics are based on end user's perspective.

5. The data represents dynamic nature of user density within an area. For example, people carry their smartphones as they move around and visit a large number of wireless/cellular access points in different locations [39].

6. Network information can be measured on an ongoing, continuous basis.

2.1.2.2 Minimization of Drive Test

Minimization of Drive Test (MDT) was introduced in 3GPP Release 10 and 11 specification to use crowdsourcing [38] to increase network performance and quality and decrease maintenance costs [17]. MDT use cases include coverage optimization, mobility optimization, capacity optimization, parametrization for common channels, and quality of service (QoS) verification [17] [26] [38]. Chernogorov et al. [26] [27] used MDT with radio measurements (i.e., Reference Signal Received Power (RSRP), Channel Quality Indicator (CQI), etc.) and KPIs (i.e., throughput, Constant BitRate, etc.) to estimate users' QoS level. Furthermore, Rodriguez and Bressan [81] proposed an MDT solution with radio frequency (RF) parameters and Mean Opinion

Score (MOS) index to assess voice call quality of GSM network in Brazil. Finally, Dalakas [32] proposed an architecture for MDT to automatically collect, analyze, and visualize network specific KPIs for QoE provisioning.

2.1.2.3 Smartphone-based Applications

Several studies are conducted with smartphone-based crowdsourcing applications where QoS measurements are collected through a measurement suite installed on a representative sample of users' devices. Faggiani et al. [39] built a smartphone-based crowdsourcing system called Portolan. The authors distributed the Portolan app to 100 users in Italy and analyzed the quality of signal of different network operators based on device-side network measurements (i.e., Received Signal Strength). Furthermore, Poncela et al. [73] implemented a mobile-based Android service to analyze user-perceived quality by measuring QoS parameters such as round trip time and SMS delay measurements. Moreover, Mushtaq et al. [68] presented a crowdsourcing framework to measure QoS parameters such as packet loss, delay, jitter, and throughput of online video streaming, as perceived by the end-users. Additionally, Mojisola and Gbolahan [67] designed a crowdsourcing platform to measure QoS parameters as experienced by the end-users and compared against the KPI benchmarks set by the Nigerian Communications Commission. Finally, Casas et al. [24] used crowdsourcing to obtain QoS/QoE measurements of end-users and used machine learning to predict QoE in smartphones for mobile apps such as YouTube, Facebook, and Google Maps.

2.1.2.4 Open Source Tools

Currently, there are open source software applications available to measure network performance based on information collected through end-user mobile devices. Tools such as Mobilyzer [70], Mobiperf [45] and Netalyzer [56] help measure device-side QoS parameters. Mobilyzer can be deployed as a library for Android apps, Mobiperf can be run on Android and iOS devices, and Netalyzer can be executed as a Java applet on a web browser.

2.2 Factors Affecting QoS

The following factors affect network performance at an end-user level:

1. Placement of cellular towers and wireless access points within a city.

2. User density and usage patterns around cellular towers and wireless access points.

3. Network service demand of mobile applications.

4. Network-tuning.

Studying subscribers' data usage and mobility patterns can help a network service provider optimize the network and improve end-user experience through network-tuning and other means.

2.2.1 Estimating User Density to Improve End-User Experience

To improve network performance, location information of mobile devices can be used by mobile service providers for estimating the spatial density of network subscribers. Halepovic and Williamson [44] analyzed 3G network cellular data of 4,156 users from a one-week duration to model user mobility patterns based on data traffic traces. The authors of [44] studied the quality of service of the network by exploring mobility events, roaming range, load across the cell sites, and correlation between call activity and user mobility. Xu et al. [96] derived a model which combined time, location of towers, and traffic frequency spectrum to extract traffic patterns around 3G and LTE towers. Based on one-month data usage information of 150,000 wireless subscribers in China, the authors of [96] grouped traffic patterns into residence, office, entertainment, transport, and comprehensive. Also, the authors of [96] suggested that the traffic of any arbitrary cellular tower could be constructed as a linear combination of four primary components corresponding to human behavior. Lee et al. [59] proposed a Dirichlet Process mixture model to integrate mobile device location information, as collected over a year in the Florida Keys, to estimate the spatial density of mobile devices for network capacity planning.

2.2.1.1 Population Distribution

Numerous studies have estimated population density within a city using mobile phone data for the purpose of city planning, transportation scheduling, emergency response to natural disasters, etc. These studies are not directly related to network quality management to improve end-user QoS, but the findings presented are useful in the context of user density estimation. For example, Ricciato et al. [80], Xu et al. [97], Deville et al. [35], and Khodabandelou et al. [54] derived a model using mobile network data to estimate dynamic population distribution in a geographic area. Also, Zhang et al. used kernel density estimation (KDE) and convolutional long short-term memory model to estimate and predict the spatial and temporal distribution of mobile phone users in China [101].

2.2.2 Usage Patterns of Mobile Subscribers

Characterizing user behavior and usage patterns within a network can help a service provider fine-tune the network and offer a personalized service to end-users to help improve their experience. Shafiq et al. studied large-scale mobile usage data in the US and derived a model to capture the volume dynamics of Internet traffic [85]. The authors discovered that 5% of the devices were responsible for 90% of the network traffic and 10% of the applications accounted for more than 99% of the flows [85]. Also, the authors found that the distribution of traffic volume with respect to applications varied for different device types [85].

Paul et al. [71] analyzed data from the nationwide 3G network and found that less than 10% of subscribers generated 90% of the load, and 10% of base stations carried 50-60% of the load. The authors [71] noticed that a large fraction of subscribers moved within one mile distance and effective bit rate was poorer for low volume users than high volume users due to the types of applications they used. Jin et al. [47] examined 3G cellular networks in the US and learned that the small number of heavy users (i.e, consume data on the order of magnitude more than normal users) were the main driving factor behind traffic volume variation in the network. The authors [47] found that heavy users concentrated on a small number of network activities such as video/audio streaming and social network access. Li et al. [61] investigated service usage patterns in 3G and 4G cellular networks in China and noticed that 98% of the network users consumed less than 500 Mbits of data with downlink traffic being higher than uplink traffic. The authors of [61] stated that users with more mobility generated less data traffic as they used applications with less traffic demand such as web browsing and instant messages during their travel and used high-traffic applications such as videos in a fixed location.

2.2.2.1 Mobile Application Usage

Network user behavior based on mobile application usage, as studied by Silva et al. [88] using smartphone data from mobile users in Brazil, indicated that social media applications such as Facebook demand a high network load, given the usage frequency and multimedia capabilities. Yang et al. [99] studied mobile user behavior for application usage in China and concluded that heavy users, comprising top 1% of user traffic, tend to consume more data on the app store, online gaming, and music. Bohmer et al. [20] conducted a study on Android mobile users in the United States and Europe and determined that news applications are popular in the mornings and game applications at nights while communication applications remain in use throughout the day.

2.2.3 Placement of Cell Towers and Wireless Access Points

One of the challenging tasks for a network service provider is to determine where to locate the cellular towers so that each user in the service area receives a sufficiently high quality of service. Amaldi et al. [12] investigated mathematical programming models to optimize the location and configuration of cellular towers in 3G networks by taking into account both uplink and downlink directions. Furthermore, Singh et al. [89] designed and implemented a fuzzy logic system, based on an extensive survey and input parameters such as end-user density, to select an accurate location for cell tower installation. Moreover, Karulkar [51] used geographic information systems software and non-linear programming to find an optimal location of a cellular tower in the network. Finally, Qiu et al. [75] deployed 802.11ax-based WiFi network with the goal of using a minimum number of access points to fulfill users' throughput requirement.

2.2.4 Network Performance Tuning

Network performance tuning aims at providing the end-user with a quality of experience suitable for the desired service [65]. Magnusson and Oom [63] proposed a prototype consisting of distributed architecture and a self-tuning algorithm to improve the capacity and quality of the cellular network. Furthermore, Shafiq et al. [86] studied cellular network performance during sporting events and suggested that tuning of radio resource allocation mitigated the effects of network performance degradation.

Moreover, Mismar et al. developed an automated cellular network-tuning framework using reinforcement learning to improve the end-user QoE in a network with impairments and faults [65].

2.3 Chapter Summary

Previous studies have demonstrated a small-scale analysis of a network's quality of service. For example, the traditional drive testing method, used to assess a network's QoS, is performed over a small geographic area for widely separated time intervals. One of the disadvantages of this method is that it provides a static view of a network's performance.

This **book** focuses on analyzing crowdsourced mobile data with device-side QoS measurements, which provides a dynamic, user-centric view of the network performance. This information is beneficial to the network operators as the data covers a large geographical area and represents spatial-temporal information of mobile users (i.e., how users access the mobile network in a region over a continuous period). The main difference and distinction of this **book** with prior work is the scale and density of the available device-side QoS data, i.e., orders of magnitude larger than has been used in prior studies. While prior literature has examples of analysis of large-scale mobile network data, it is mainly used to predict cellular traffic [92] and extract traffic patterns [96]. However, this **book** uses the device-side QoS measurements to determine how the user densities change in a geographic area over time and whether the user densities have an impact on end-user QoS levels in the mobile network.

Chapter 3

Description Of Mobile Network Data And Pre-Processing Steps

The crowd-sourced QoS mobile network data [7] analyzed in this book is from a large metropolitan area, collected over five months, from August 1, 2018, to December 31, 2018. The data consisted of device-side QoS measurements recorded daily from approximately 10,000 to 50,000 user devices. Figure 3.1 shows the device count from August 1, 2018, to December 31, 2018, divided into a sequence of biweekly periods. For August 1-14, the device count for each day remains consistent; however, it increases for August 15-31 and September 1-14 (i.e., toward the end of the period). Furthermore, the device count remains steady throughout September 15-30 and October 1-14, but it starts to increase during the end of October 15-31 and November 1-14. From November 14, 2018, to December 31, 2018, the device count increases by a factor of five as compared to August 1-14.

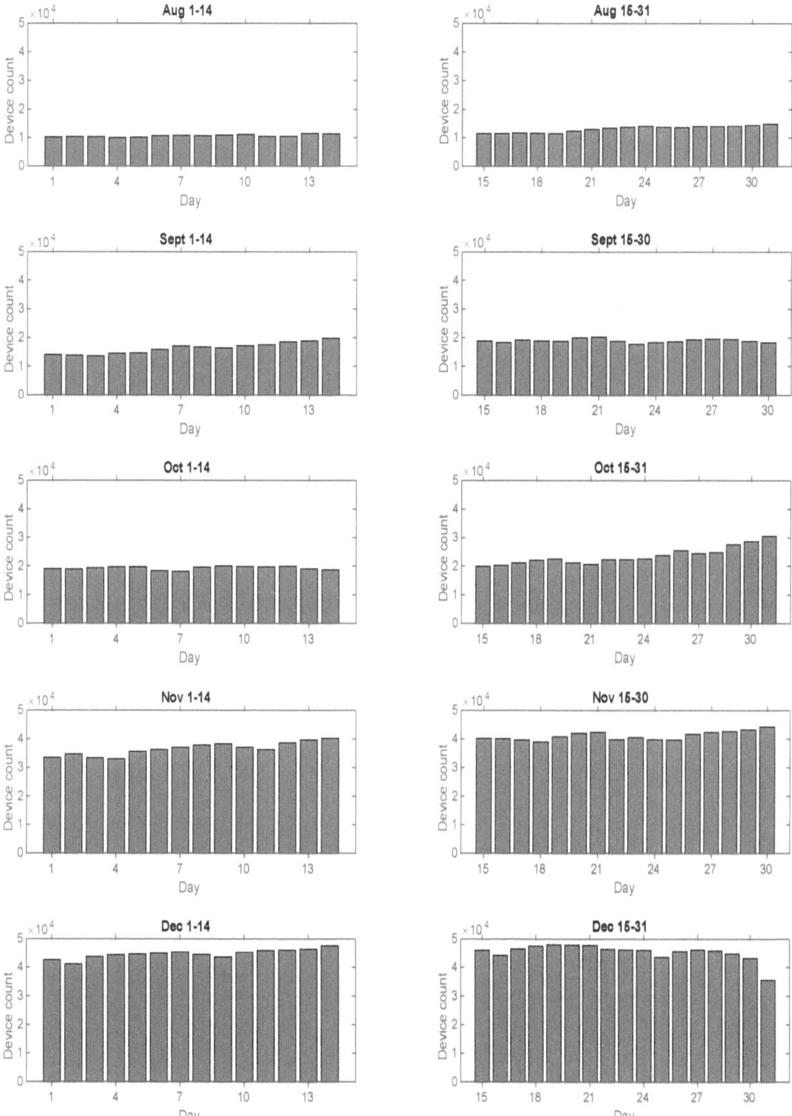

Figure 3.1: Bar plot showing device count from August 1, 2018, to December 31, 2018, broken into a sequence of biweekly periods. Each bar represents a day of a month within the five-month period with a corresponding number of user devices used for device-side measurements.

3.1   Data Collection

The mobile network data, provided by Tutela Technologies Inc. [7], consisted of the following information:

1. Location information of user devices.

2. QoS measurements of user devices.

3. Timestamps related to QoS measurements.

3.1.1   Location, QoS Parameters, and Timestamp

The data consisted of users from a densely populated region, i.e., Manhattan, and contained data fields (i.e., data columns) such as Location_Latitude and Location_Longitude, which represented GPS coordinates of a user device's location. The data included locations of user devices within twenty-five miles of Manhattan latitude and longitude coordinates. Figure 3.2 shows 500,000 data observations from August 1, 2018, to August 14, 2018, where each observation corresponds to latitude and longitude of user devices. The data also contained QoS measurements for user devices (see Table 3.1 for a description [8]).

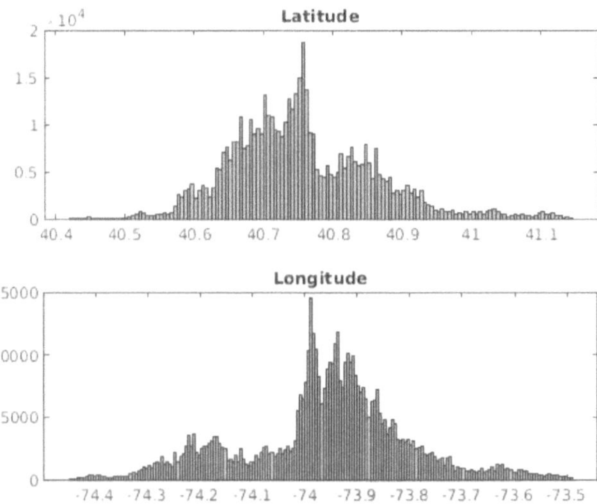

Figure 3.2: Histogram showing 500,000 observations from August 1, 2018, to August 14, 2018. Each observation corresponds to the latitude and longitude of user devices in the Manhattan area.

QoS Parameter	Description	Range/Units
QoS_CQI	Channel Quality Indicator (LTE network)	Integer
QoS_Delta_Received_Bytes	The received bytes over the wireless radio since the last QoS measurement was taken on the same device and connection	bytes
QoS_Delta_Transmitted_Bytes	The transmitted bytes over the wireless radio since the last QoS measurement was taken on the same device and connection	bytes
QoS_DownloadThroughput	The measured download throughput, as calculated by measuring the duration it takes to download a 2MB file from the test server	kbps
QoS_UploadThroughput	The upload throughput, as calculated by measuring the duration it takes to upload a 1MB file to the test server over a TCP connection	kbps
QoS_JitterAverage	The average measured jitter (packet delay variation)	ms
QoS_JitterMin	The minimum measured jitter (packet delay variation)	ms
QoS_LatencyAverage	The average measured latency, calculated as half of the round-trip duration of sending 20 UDP packets to a test server.	ms
QoS_LatencyMin	The minimum measured latency on the current wireless connection	ms
QoS_LinkSpeed	The connected Wi-Fi wireless access point link speed or theoretical maximum data received throughput	Mbps
QoS_LinkUpstreamBandwidth	The estimated first hop upstream (device to network) bandwidth	kbps
QoS_LinkDownstreamBandwidth	The estimated first hop downstream (network to device) bandwidth	kbps
QoS_PacketLossDiscardPercentage	The measured packet discard on the current wireless connection	0 - 1
QoS_PacketLossLostPercentage	The measured packet loss, as calculated by measuring the number of UDP packets that do not complete the round-trip from the device to a test server and back	0 - 1
QoS_RSRP	Reference Signal Received Power (measures signal level of LTE network)	dBm
QoS_RSRQ	Reference Signal Received Quality (measures signal quality of LTE network)	dB
QoS_RSSNR	Reference signal signal to noise ratio (LTE network)	0.1 db
QoS_SignalStrength	Signal Strength (2G, 3G, 4G, LTE network)	dBm
QoS_SignalLevel	Abstract signal level value for the overall signal strength and quality	0-4
QoS_TA	Mobile Timing Advance (LTE or GSM)	Integer

Table 3.1: Description of data fields representing QoS parameters.

Finally, the data included timestamp information such as QoS_Date, which corresponds to the time the QoS measurements were taken for a user device. Figure 3.3 shows a histogram with 500,000 observations from August 1, 2018, to August 14, 2018, where each observation corresponds to the timestamp the QoS measurements were taken for a user device. The histogram has a bin size of 8 hours, and the vertical dashed lines mark the end of each day. Note, more QoS measurements were taken after evenings (i.e., after 4 p.m.) than mornings or afternoons each day.

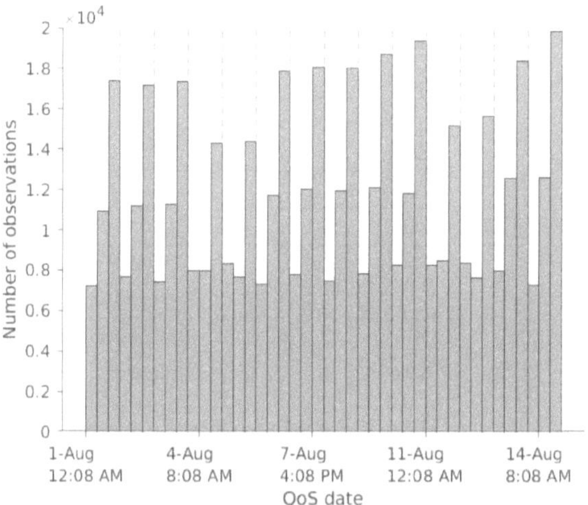

Figure 3.3: Histogram represents 500,000 observations from August 1, 2018, to August 14, 2018. Each observation corresponds to the timestamp the QoS measurements were taken for a user device. Each bin size is 8 hours and the red vertical lines represent the end of each day.

As the goal of this **book** is to study user densities over time, the mobile network data was collected from August 1, 2018, to December 31, 2018, and divided into a sequence of biweekly periods. Additionally, due to data having a high volume, the biweekly periods from October 15th onward were divided into multiple shards. Table 3.2 shows the biweekly periods between August 1, 2018, to December 31, 2018, with a total number of observations for each period. Each observation contains location coordinates, QoS measurements, and timestamp information (i.e., the time when QoS measurements were taken) for a user device.

Biweekly periods Year: 2018	Number of shards	Number of observations	
Aug 1 - Aug 14	1		25,035,210
Aug 15 - Aug 31	1		37,765,887
Sept 1 - Sept 14	1		33,483,751
Sept 15 - Sept 30	1		41,692,073
Oct 1 - Oct 14	1		37,392,284
Oct 15 - Oct 31	2	shard 1:	30,553,844
		shard 2:	30,540,063
Nov 1 - Nov 14	3	shard 1:	29,813,222
		shard 2:	29,814,143
		shard 3:	23,857,242
Nov 15 - Nov 30	4	shard 1:	30,429,549
		shard 2:	30,429,513
		shard 3:	30,425,249
		shard 4:	35,748,502
Dec 1 - Dec 14	4	shard 1:	29,811,980
		shard 2:	29,796,526
		shard 3:	29,805,881
		shard 4:	32,029,345
Dec 15 - Dec 31	4	shard 1:	33,419,805
		shard 2:	33,423,213
		shard 3:	33,416,441
		shard 4:	39,266,267
Total			707,949,990

Table 3.2: The dataset corresponding to biweekly periods from August 1, 2018, to December 31, 2018. Each biweekly period has number of observations, where each observation consists of timestamp, location, and QoS measurement information of a user device. The biweekly period from October 15th onward contains multiple shards.

3.1.2 Database Query

The query used to retrieve the data contained the following conditions:

1. The QoS_Date spanned the sequence of biweekly periods between August 1, 2018, to December 31, 2018.

2. Location_Latitude and Location_Longitude were within a twenty-five mile radius of Manhattan coordinates, 40.7831 latitude and -73.9712 longitude.

Figure 3.4 shows a geographic map with 500,000 observations from August 1, 2018, to August 14, 2018, where each observation corresponds to the latitude and longitude coordinates of user devices within twenty-five miles of Manhattan coordinates.

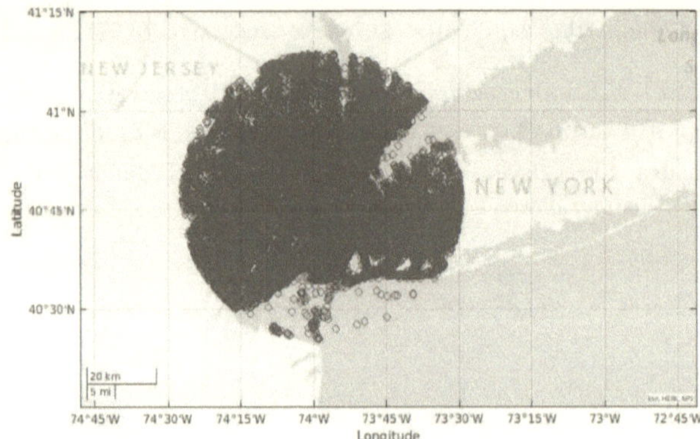

(a) Geographic map showing latitude and longitude of user devices (blue dots) falling within a twenty-five mile radius of Manhattan latitude and longitude coordinates.

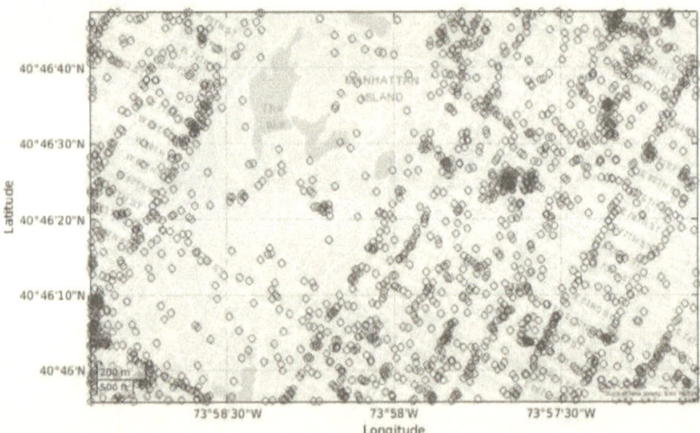

(b) A zoomed-in street view of Manhattan island with latitude and longitude of user devices (blue dots).

Figure 3.4: Data with 500,000 observations from August 1, 2018, to August 14, 2018. Each observation represents the latitude and longitude of a user device within a twenty-five mile radius of Manhattan latitude and longitude coordinates (blue dots).

The twenty-five mile distance from Manhattan coordinates was calculated using the **Great Circle Distance**, which calculates the shortest distance between two points on a sphere [23] [29] [2]. The two points lie on a unique great circle, which has the same center and radius as the sphere, and the shortest path between the points forms an arc (see Figure 3.5).

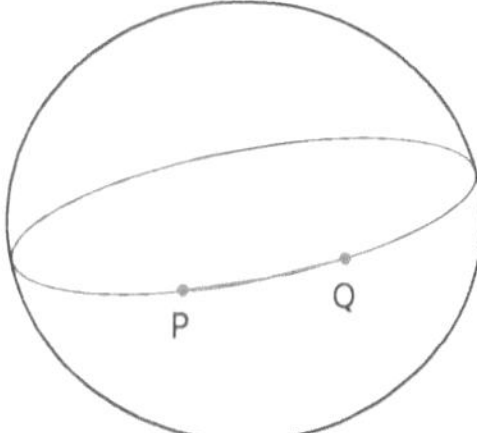

Figure 3.5: Great circle with an arc containing points P and Q.

Equations 3.1 and 3.2 show the Great Circle Distance calculation between two points [29]. Equation 3.1 was used to calculate the angle between two points:

$$\theta = arccos\left(sin\phi_1 sin\phi_2 + cos\phi_1 cos\phi_2 cos\left(\lambda_1 - \lambda_2\right)\right) \tag{3.1}$$

where θ is the angle measure between point one and point two, ϕ_1 is the point one latitude (i.e., user device latitude), ϕ_2 is the point two latitude, (i.e., Manhattan latitude), λ_1 is point 1 longitude (i.e., user device longitude), and λ_2 is point two longitude (i.e., Manhattan longitude). Note, θ, latitude, and longitude were measured in radians. Equation 3.2 was used to convert the angle θ, from Equation 3.1, to distance in miles:

$$d = \theta R \tag{3.2}$$

where d is the Great Circle Distance between two points in miles, θ is the angle measure between two points in radians, and R is the radius of the Earth equal to 3959 miles. Equation 3.1 [29] is based on an underlying assumption that the Earth is a sphere. Hence, it has an error of 1% when calculating a distance above 100 km due to the Earth being an ellipsoid [23]. However, the extracted data has user devices located within a distance of 25 miles (40 km) from the Manhattan coordinates, thus making the error negligible. Also, Equation 3.1 assumes that the surface of the Earth is smooth and therefore does not correct for elevation. Appendix A.1 shows the SQL query for retrieving the data based on QoS_Date, Location_Latitude, and Location_Longitude. Note, the QoS_Date is from August 01, 2018, to August 14, 2018, one of the biweekly periods that the five month's duration was divided into (see Table

3.2). Also, Location_Latitude and Location_Longitude of user devices are based on the Great Circle Distance and lie within 25 miles of Manhattan latitude and longitude coordinates.

3.2 Data Pre-processing

For each biweekly period between August 1, 2018, to December 31, 2018, the data was pre-processed to convert it to a numerical format for an efficient analysis in Matlab. The pre-processing steps involved:

1. Data Standardization.

2. Data Validation.

3. Data Mapping and Conversion.

3.2.1 Data Standardization

The mobile network data contained four different data types: integer, float, string, and timestamp (UTC) (see Tutela's documentation [8]). Data fields with a float data type were standardized to ensure they had a consistent representation, format, and precision. The measurements recorded by mobile devices as a float or a double have a representation of a 32-bit or 64-bit IEEE floating-point in Matlab. The significant digits in the measured values were *less* than the digits represented by an IEEE floating-point. Hence, the data fields with a float data type required a truncation. Location_Latitude and Location_Longitude were truncated to contain 6 decimal places as the resolution was sufficient to represent information about a user device's geolocation in a city. In general, GPS devices are accurate up to 6 decimal places and have a resolution of a city block within a city core. Furthermore, QoS_UploadThroughput, QoS_DownloadThroughput, QoS_LatencyMin, QoS_LatencyAverage, and QoS_JitterAverage were also truncated to contain 6 decimal places as the precision was sufficient to represent the QoS parameters. Finally, QoS_PacketLossDiscardPercentage and QoS_PacketLossLostPercentage were truncated to 2 decimal places as they represented percentages. Table 3.3 shows the data fields with float data types truncated to their respective decimal places.

Data Field	Number of Decimal Places	Range/Units
Location_Latitude	6	-90 to 90
Location_Longitude	6	-180 to 180
QoS_UploadThroughput	6	kbps
QoS_DownloadThroughput	6	kbps
QoS_LatencyMin	6	ms
QoS_LatencyAverage	6	ms
QoS_JitterAverage	6	ms
QoS_PacketLossDiscardPercentage	2	0 - 1
QoS_PacketLossLostPercentage	2	0 - 1

Table 3.3: Data fields stored as an IEEE floating point were truncated to the respective number of decimal places.

The data field, QoS_JitterMin, stored measurements in a scientific notation. The IEEE-754 floating point standard for 64-bit numbers allocates 1 bit for sign, 11 bits for the exponent, and 52 bits for the mantissa [77]. The highest precision of the mantissa for a 64-bit number in IEEE-754 floating point standard is $4.5 * 10^{15}$ in a decimal representation. To preserve the precision of measurements stored in the QoS_JitterMin field, the scientific notation was split into the coefficient and the exponent and stored in QoS_Jitter_Min_Coefficient and QoS_Jitter_Min_Exponent respectively. Table 3.4 shows QoS_JitterMin data in a scientific notation and the splitting of coefficient and exponent to store them separately.

Scientific Notation QoS_JitterMin		Coefficient QoS_Jitter_Min_Coefficient	Exponent QoS_Jitter_Min_Exponent
1e-12		1.000000	-12
1e12	<- splits ->	1.000000	12
4.2e06		4.200000	6
-4.70e+9		-4.700000	9
4.2e-06		4.200000	-6

Table 3.4: QoS_JitterMin, as represented using scientific notation, was split to store coefficient and exponent separately in QoS_Jitter_Min_Coefficient and QoS_Jitter_Min_Exponent data fields.

Data fields with a string data type consisted of four types of values: double-quoted empty string, double-quoted string, string, and an empty string. The double-quoted empty string represented an *unset* value, i.e., the user device did not record the value for a data field. On the other hand, an empty value represented an *unknown* value, i.e., the value for a data field could not be retrieved from the user's device. To properly represent both value types and distinguish their meaning, the double-quoted empty string was replaced with **Not Set**. The rest of the string values remained the same.

3.2.2 Data Validation

As the data was high volume, a validation step was performed to ensure the data had a proper format and precision, a consistent representation, and remained intact after standardization. To verify the data had a correct number of columns, i.e., no column was accidentally deleted, each row in the dataset was checked against a specified number (i.e., 112 columns). Also, the data fields with the float data type such as the ones listed in Table 3.3, QoS_Jitter_Min_Coefficient, and QoS_Jitter_Min_Exponent were validated as follows:

1. The data field name (i.e., column name) and its position were checked to ensure the columns were not swapped or deleted.

2. Each value in the data field (i.e., data column) was checked for a proper format and a correct number of decimal places.

After examining the error logs for the standardization and validation steps, it was concluded that the data from August 1, 2018, to December 31, 2018, had a correct format and precision, a consistent representation, and proper columns.

3.2.3 Data Mapping and Conversion

The raw data was standardized and stored in an intermediate text file which was then validated to ensure data consistency. As mentioned earlier, the data consisted of four data types: integer, float, timestamp (UTC), and string. Both string and timestamp data types were converted to a numerical format for efficient data analysis. The data fields with the timestamp data type were converted from a datetime format to a Unix timestamp format. Furthermore, to convert the data fields with a string data type to a numerical format, each value was mapped to a corresponding number (i.e., 0, 1, 2, 3, etc). Note, the duplicated values within a data field had the same numerical mapping. Also, multiple entries representing the same information within a data field followed the same numerical mapping. For example, "New York" and

"new york" refer to the same city and thus mapped to the same number. Finally, as
there are multiple datasets corresponding to biweekly periods, the repetitive entries
of a data field also consisted of the same numerical mapping. To ensure consistency,
string-to-number mappings were stored as *metadata*, which was used and updated
during pre-processing of datasets. As mentioned in Subsection 3.2.1, the data fields
with string data type contained double-quoted empty strings, which were replaced
with **Not Set**, and empty strings. Values containing **Not Set** were mapped to 0
and empty strings were mapped to NaNs. Note, the data fields with float and integer
data types also contained empty values, which were replaced with NaNs. Listing
3.1 shows an example of metadata with string-to-number mapping for data fields
Device_Language and Device_SIMServiceProvider. Note, Device_SIMServiceProvider
has *not set* mapped to 0 and empty string mapped to NaN. Before the mapping
and conversion step, each data field was checked for its data type. If a value for a
data field contained an incorrect data type, the entire row containing the value was
discarded. The data was then stored as a Matlab file (i.e., pre-processed file) and
used for further analysis.

```
Device_Language:
{'not set': 0, 'en': 1, 'es': 2, 'bg': 3, 'fr': 4,
'ko': 5, 'pt': 6, 'zh': 7, 'vi': 8, 'nxt_val': 9}


Device_SIMServiceProvider:
{'not set': 0, 'metropcs': 1, 'sprint': 2,
'u.s. cellular': 3, 'virgin mobile': 4, 'mobilenation': 5,
'nxt_val': 54, '': nan}
```

Listing 3.1: An example of metadata containing string-to-number mapping for Device_Language
and Device_SIMServiceProvider.

3.3 Verification of Pre-Processed Data

To verify the mapping and conversion step, the pre-processed data was transformed
back and compared with the intermediate text file, produced during the standardization step (Subsection 3.2.1). The following steps outline the verification process:

1. Data fields with Unix timestamp format were transformed back to the datetime
   format (UTC).

2. Data fields with numerical mappings were transformed back to string data type. The values in the data fields were mapped back to their original string values using the metadata, which has string-to-number mapping (mentioned in Subsection 3.2.3). Note, values with 0 were mapped back to **Not Set** and NaNs were changed to empty strings.

3. Data fields with float data type were reformatted to contain a specific number of decimal places as Matlab stores 64-bit floating point numbers using the IEEE-754 floating point standard. For example, Matlab stores 26.618775 as 26.618774999999999. The precision of the floating point values stored in Matlab is higher than precision used in standardization for data fields with float data type (see Table 3.3). Hence, the data fields were reformatted for easier comparison.

4. Data fields with integer and float data type contained values with NaNs, which were changed to empty values.

Table 3.5 shows an example of transforming data fields back to their standardized values to verify the mapping and conversion step. Device_Language, which has numerical mappings, was mapped to its original string values using the metadata. Location_Latitude, which has a float data type, was reformatted to contain 6 decimal places (as specified in Table 3.3). QoS_Date, which has a Unix timestamp format, was changed back to the datetime (UTC) format.

Device_Language	Location_Latitude	QoS_Date
1	26.618774999999999	1.5520631940000000e+09
1	26.558097000000000	1.5524560680000000e+09
1	26.558116999999999	1.5524353490000000e+09
1	26.55802500000000	1.5524612830000000e+09

Device_Language	Location_Latitude	QoS_Date
en	26.618775	2019-03-08 16:39:54 UTC
en	26.558097	2019-03-13 05:47:48 UTC
en	26.558117	2019-03-13 00:02:29 UTC
en	26.558025	2019-03-13 07:14:43 UTC

Table 3.5: An example of transforming data fields to verify the mapping and conversion step. The top table shows data that has been pre-processed (i.e., standardized, validated, and gone through mapping and conversion steps). The bottom table shows the data transformed back to its standardized values.

The transformed data was then compared with the intermediate text file, produced during the standardization step (i.e., before the data was mapped and converted). It was concluded that the data mapping and conversion step successfully converted the standardized data into a numerical format without introducing errors and keeping the data quality intact.

3.4 Data Pipeline

The data pipeline (Figure 3.6) summarizes the flow of data through the pre-processing and verification steps.

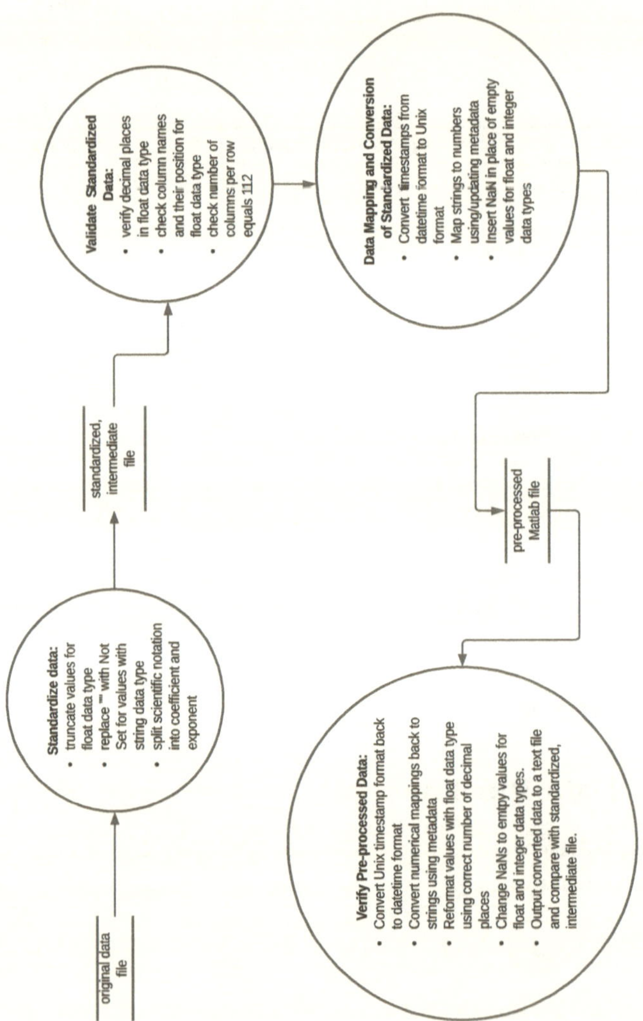

Figure 3.6: Overview of the data flow.

3.5   Chapter Summary

Mobile network data contained information such as location coordinates of user devices, QoS measurements of user devices, and timestamps related to QoS measurements. Locations of user devices were selected to be within a twenty-five mile radius of Manhattan latitude and longitude coordinates. Furthermore, the data spanned from August 1, 2018, to December 31, 2018, based on the timestamps for QoS measurements. During pre-processing, the raw data was first standardized and validated to ensure it had a correct format and precision, a consistent representation, and a proper number of columns. The data was then mapped and converted to a numerical format for efficient analysis. To verify the mapping and conversion step, the data was transformed back to its standardized values and compared with the intermediate text file, produced during the standardization step.

Chapter 4

Mobile Subscriber Density in a Network

Device-side QoS measurements are useful in analyzing end-user experience in a mobile network. These measurements provide information about user density and usage patterns over time, which helps a network carrier design and maintain a cellular network and improve the end-user experience. The crowd-sourced mobile network data [7] analyzed in this book contains device-side QoS measurements from a densely populated area, i.e., Manhattan, with a duration of five months. To extract user density estimates from the available mobile device QoS data, the following algorithms were combined:

1. Kernel Density Estimation (KDE) - for the estimation of the probability density function.

2. Expectation Maximization (EM) - for the estimation of Gaussian (i.e., Normal) kernels for the KDE.

4.1   Kernel Density Estimation

Kernel Density Estimation (KDE) is a non-parametric technique used to estimate an unknown probability density function (PDF). Equation 4.1 [37] shows the general KDE formula:

$$p(\boldsymbol{x}) = \frac{1}{K} \sum_{k=1}^{K} \frac{1}{V_k} \varphi \left(\frac{\boldsymbol{x} - \boldsymbol{x}_k}{h_k} \right) \tag{4.1}$$

where $\varphi()$ is a kernel function (also known as a window function), V_k is the volume of the kernel function, $\mathbf{x}_k$ and h_k are the parameters of the kernel function with $\boldsymbol{x}_k$ as the center of the kernel and h_k as the width of the kernel, K is the number of kernels, and $\boldsymbol{x}$ is a sample observation. Note, $\left(\dfrac{\boldsymbol{x}-\boldsymbol{x}_k}{h_k}\right)$ normalizes the sample observation $\boldsymbol{x}$ with respect to the kernel center $\boldsymbol{x}_k$ and kernel width h_k. As there are multiple K kernels, the factor $\left(\dfrac{1}{K}\right)$ further normalizes the sample observation $\boldsymbol{x}$. The sample observations, $\boldsymbol{x}$, represent latitude and longitude of user devices from the mobile network data, as shown in Table 3.2. As a sum of Gaussians can be used to estimate any probability density function (i.e., Gaussian kernels form a basis set for any PDF) [41], the kernel function used for the KDE was chosen to be a bivariate Normal density function shown in Equation 4.2:

$$\varphi(\boldsymbol{x}) = \frac{1}{(2\pi)^{d/2}|\hat{\boldsymbol{\Sigma}}_k|^{1/2}} exp\left[-\frac{1}{2}(\boldsymbol{x}-\hat{\boldsymbol{\mu}}_k)^t\hat{\boldsymbol{\Sigma}}_k^{-1}(\boldsymbol{x}-\hat{\boldsymbol{\mu}}_k)\right] \tag{4.2}$$

where $\boldsymbol{x}$ is a sample observation mentioned above, $d = 2$ is the number of dimensions (i.e., latitude and longitude), k is the index of a particular kernel, $\hat{\boldsymbol{\Sigma}}_k$ and $\hat{\boldsymbol{\mu}}_k$ are respectively, the estimated sample covariance and mean of the kth kernel, as estimated via Expectation Maximization (EM) applied to the QoS data latitude and longitude measurement features (described in Section 4.2). Note, $\hat{\boldsymbol{\mu}}_k$ represents the center of the Normal density kernel and corresponds to the $\boldsymbol{x}_k$ of the general KDE formula (Equation 4.1). Similarly, the normalization constant $\left(\dfrac{1}{(2\pi)^{d/2}|\hat{\boldsymbol{\Sigma}}_k|^{1/2}}\right)$, which ensures the kernel has a unity integral over the domain $(-\infty, \infty)$, corresponds to $\left(\dfrac{1}{h_k}\right)$ of the general KDE formula (Equation 4.1). The volume, V_k, corresponds to the integral of the Gaussian kernel, which is equal to 1. The kernels are scaled appropriately to ensure $p(\boldsymbol{x})$ is a proper probability density function and meets the following Kolmogorov's axioms of probability [37]:

$$P(A) \geq 0 \tag{4.3}$$

$$P(S) = 1 \tag{4.4}$$

$$P(A \cup B) = P(A) + P(B) \tag{4.5}$$

where S is the sample space (i.e., the set of all possible outcomes), A is any event in the sample space S, and A and B are disjoint events in the sample space S.

Algorithm 4.1 shows the KDE pseudocode. The algorithm estimates the probability of each sample observation, $\boldsymbol{x}_i$, using $\hat{\boldsymbol{\mu}}_k$ and $\hat{\boldsymbol{\Sigma}}_k$ for each kth kernel. The algorithm then normalizes the probabilities by the weight of each kth kernel. The criterion for choosing K kernels is discussed in Section 4.4.

Algorithm 4.1: Pseudocode for KDE algorithm.

```
// @x:  bivariate data
// @K:  number of kernels
// @μ̂_K:  contains μ̂ for K kernels
// @Σ̂_K:  contains Σ̂ for K kernels
// @w_K:  contains weights of K kernels
```

Function KDE($\boldsymbol{x}$, $\hat{\boldsymbol{\mu}}_K$, $\hat{\boldsymbol{\Sigma}}_K$, w_K, K):

    n = length($\boldsymbol{x}$) // number of observations

    $Px = [\,]$ // stores estimated probability values for x

    for $i = 1$ *to* n **do**

        $\boldsymbol{x}_i = \boldsymbol{x}(i)$ // each data observation

        $p = 0$

        for $k = 1$ *to* K **do**

            $\hat{\boldsymbol{\mu}}_k = \hat{\boldsymbol{\mu}}_K(\mathrm{k})$ // mean of kth kernel

            $\hat{\boldsymbol{\Sigma}}_k = \hat{\boldsymbol{\Sigma}}_K(\mathrm{k})$ // covariance of kth kernel

            $w_k = w_K(\mathrm{k})$ // weight of kth kernel

            // estimated probability of $\boldsymbol{x}_i$

$$p_k = \frac{1}{(2\pi)|\hat{\boldsymbol{\Sigma}}_k|^{1/2}} exp\left[-\frac{1}{2}(\boldsymbol{x}_i - \hat{\boldsymbol{\mu}}_k)^t \hat{\boldsymbol{\Sigma}}_k^{-1}(\boldsymbol{x}_i - \hat{\boldsymbol{\mu}}_k)\right]$$

            $p_w = w_k * p_k$ // adjust the probability of x of kth kernel by its weight

            $p = p + p_w$ //

        $Px = $ append(Px, p)

    return Px

4.2 Expectation Maximization

Expectation Maximization (EM) was used to estimate the parameters $\hat{\boldsymbol{\mu}}_k$, $\hat{\boldsymbol{\Sigma}}_k$, and w_k of Gaussian kernels. EM uses the Bayes rule (Equation 4.6) to estimate $\hat{\boldsymbol{\mu}}_k$, $\hat{\boldsymbol{\Sigma}}_k$, and w_k, where the likelihood, $P(\boldsymbol{x}_i|k)$, is calculated using the Gaussian PDF (Equation 4.7),

$$P(k|\boldsymbol{x}_i) = \frac{P(\boldsymbol{x}_i|k) * P(k)}{\sum_{k=1}^{K} P(\boldsymbol{x}_i|k) * P(k)} \tag{4.6}$$

$$P(\boldsymbol{x}_i|k) = \frac{1}{(2\pi)^{d/2}|\hat{\boldsymbol{\Sigma}}_k|^{1/2}} exp\left[-\frac{1}{2}(\boldsymbol{x}_i - \hat{\boldsymbol{\mu}}_k)^t \hat{\boldsymbol{\Sigma}}_k^{-1}(\boldsymbol{x}_i - \hat{\boldsymbol{\mu}}_k)\right] \tag{4.7}$$

with k as the kth kernel, d as the number of dimensions (i.e., 2), and $\boldsymbol{x}_i$ as a sample observation. Algorithm 4.2 shows the pseudocode for EM. The algorithm starts with the initialization of weights, w_K, corresponding to $P(k)$ in Equation 4.6. The algorithm then uses K-means to initialize $\hat{\boldsymbol{\mu}}_K$ and $\hat{\boldsymbol{\Sigma}}_K$. After initialization, the algorithm uses the E-step (Algorithm 4.3) to calculate the probability that the observed sample $\boldsymbol{x}_i$ came from the kth kernel. Also, the algorithm uses the M-step (Algorithm 4.4) to update the parameters $\hat{\boldsymbol{\mu}}_K$, $\hat{\boldsymbol{\Sigma}}_K$, and w_K using the calculated probabilities. As both E and M steps are iterative, the algorithm continues until the change in log-likelihood (Algorithm 4.5) reaches a threshold of $10e^{-9}$ or maximum number of iterations are completed (i.e., 3000). The EM algorithm is guaranteed to converge [34] [94]. Based on the threshold of $10e^{-9}$, the algorithm converged for the dataset corresponding to biweekly periods from August 1, 2018 to December 31, 2018 (see Table 3.2).

Algorithm 4.2: Pseudocode for EM algorithm.

```
// @x:  bivariate data
// @K:  number of kernels
```

Function EM(x, K):

$\quad$ n = length(x) // number of data observations

$\quad$ // Initialization of w_K, $\hat{\mu}_K$, and $\hat{\Sigma}_K$

$\quad$ // w_K: stores weight of each kth kernel

$\quad$ // set equal weight for each kernel, P(k)

$\quad$ $w_K = [\,]$

$\quad$ **for** $k = 1$ *to* K **do**

$\qquad$ $\lfloor$ w_K = append(w_K, 1/K)

$\quad$ //

$\quad$ // use kmeans(), Matlab defined function, to initialize $\hat{\mu}_K$ and $\hat{\Sigma}_K$

$\quad$ // $\hat{\mu}_K$: stores means of K kernels

$\quad$ // $\hat{\Sigma}_K$: stores covariances of K kernels

$\quad$ $[\hat{\mu}_K, \hat{\Sigma}_K]$ = kmeans(x, K)

$\quad$ threshold = $1.0 * 10^{-9}$ // threshold for convergence

$\quad$ maxIter = 3000 // maximum iteration, if algorithm does not converge

$\quad$ //

$\quad$ prevLogLikelihood = 0

$\quad$ currLogLikelihood = 0

$\quad$ **for** $m = 1$ *to* *maxIter* **do**

$\qquad$ // E Step

$\qquad$ // use Bayes rule to calculate posterior and evidence

$\qquad$ [posterior, evidence] = EStep(x, n, K, $\hat{\mu}_K$, $\hat{\Sigma}_K$, w_K)

$\qquad$ // M Step

$\qquad$ // update w_K, $\hat{\mu}_K$, $\hat{\Sigma}_K$

$\qquad$ $[w_K, \hat{\mu}_K, \hat{\Sigma}_K]$ = MStep(x, n, K, posterior)

$\qquad$ currLogLikelihood = computeLogLikelihood(evidence, n)

$\qquad$ // if the algorithm converges, break out of for loop

$\qquad$ diff = abs(currLogLikelihood - prevLogLikelihood)

$\qquad$ **if** *diff* $\leq$ *threshold* **then**

$\qquad\quad$ $\lfloor$ break

$\qquad$ prevLogLikelihood = currLogLikelihood
```
```

Algorithm 4.3: Pseudocode for E step of the EM algorithm.

```
/* @x: bivariate data, @n: number of data observations, @K: number of
   kernels, @μ̂_K: contains means of K kernels, @Σ_K: contains covariances
   of K kernels, @w_K: contains weights of K kernels                    */
```

Function EStep($\boldsymbol{x}$, n, K, $\hat{\boldsymbol{\mu}}_K$, $\hat{\boldsymbol{\Sigma}}_K$, w_K):

$\quad$ posterior $= []$ // stores posterior probability, $P(k|x_i)$

$\quad$ likelihood $= []$ // stores likelihood, $P(x_i|k)$

$\quad$ evidence $= []$ // stores evidence, $\sum_{k=1}^{K} P(x_i|k)*P(k)$

$\quad$ // calculate likelihood

$\quad$ **for** $k = 1$ *to* K **do**

$\quad\quad$ $l_k = []$ // store likelihood of each observation for each kth kernel

$\quad\quad$ $\hat{\boldsymbol{\mu}}_k = \hat{\boldsymbol{\mu}}_K(\mathrm{k})$ // mean of kth kernel

$\quad\quad$ $\hat{\boldsymbol{\Sigma}}_k = \hat{\boldsymbol{\Sigma}}_K(\mathrm{k})$ // covariance of kth kernel

$\quad\quad$ **for** $i = 1$ *to* n **do**

$\quad\quad\quad$ $\boldsymbol{x}_i = \boldsymbol{x}(i)$ // each data observation

$\quad\quad\quad$ $l_i = \dfrac{1}{(2\pi)|\hat{\boldsymbol{\Sigma}}_k|^{1/2}} exp\left[-\dfrac{1}{2}(\boldsymbol{x}_i - \hat{\boldsymbol{\mu}}_k)^t \hat{\boldsymbol{\Sigma}}_k^{-1}(\boldsymbol{x}_i - \hat{\boldsymbol{\mu}}_k)\right]$

$\quad\quad\quad$ $l_k = \mathrm{append}(l_k, l_i)$

$\quad\quad$ likelihood $= \mathrm{append}(\mathrm{likelihood}, l_k)$ // likelihood for all K kernels

$\quad$ // calculate evidence

$\quad$ **for** $i = 1$ *to* n **do**

$\quad\quad$ $e_i = 0$

$\quad\quad$ **for** $k = 1$ *to* K **do**

$\quad\quad\quad$ $l_{ki} = \mathrm{likelihood}(i)(k)$ // likelihood of x_i for each kth kernel

$\quad\quad\quad$ $w_k = w_K(\mathrm{k})$ // weight of kth kernel

$\quad\quad\quad$ $e_i = e_i + l_{ki} * w_k$

$\quad\quad$ evidence $= \mathrm{append}(\mathrm{evidence}, e_i)$

$\quad$ // calculate posterior

$\quad$ **for** $k = 1$ *to* K **do**

$\quad\quad$ $p_k = []$

$\quad\quad$ $w_k = w_K(\mathrm{k})$ // weight of each kth kernel

$\quad\quad$ **for** $i = 1$ *to* n **do**

$\quad\quad\quad$ $e_i = \mathrm{evidence}(i)$ // evidence of each x_i

$\quad\quad\quad$ $l_{ki} = \mathrm{likelihood}(i)(k)$ // likelihood of each x_i per k^{th} kernel

$\quad\quad\quad$ $p_i = 1/e_i * (l_{ki} * w_k)$

$\quad\quad\quad$ $p_k = \mathrm{append}(p_k, p_i)$

$\quad\quad$ posterior $= \mathrm{append}(\mathrm{posterior}, p_k)$

$\quad$ **return** *posterior, evidence*

Algorithm 4.4: Pseudocode for M step of the EM algorithm.

```
/* @x:  bivariate data, @n:  number of data observations, @K:  number of
   kernels, @posterior:  posterior probabilities of data                 */
```

Function MStep($\boldsymbol{x}$, n, K, *posterior*):

    // estimate weights, $1/n * \sum_{i=1}^{n} P(k|\boldsymbol{x}_i)$

    $w_K = []$ // store weight of K kernels

    for $k = 1$ *to* K **do**

        $w_k = 0$

        for $i = 1$ *to* n **do**

            $p_{ki} = \text{posterior(i)(k)}$ // posterior of each $\boldsymbol{x}_i$ for each kth kernel

            $w_k = w_k + p_{ki}$

        $w_k = w_k/n$

        $w_K = \text{append}(w_K, w_k)$

    // estimate mean, $\hat{\mu}_k = \dfrac{\sum_{i=1}^{n} P(k|\boldsymbol{x}_i) * \boldsymbol{x}_i}{\sum_{i=1}^{n} P(k|\boldsymbol{x}_i)}$

    $\hat{\boldsymbol{\mu}}_K = []$ // store mean of K kernels

    for $k = 1$ *to* K **do**

        $\hat{\boldsymbol{\mu}}_k = [0\ 0]$

        $p_{ki}sum = 0$ // sum of posteriors per k^{th} kernel

        for $i = 1$ *to* n **do**

            $\boldsymbol{x}_i = \boldsymbol{x}(i)$ // each data observation

            $p_{ki} = \text{posterior(i)(k)}$// posterior of each $\boldsymbol{x}_i$ for each kth kernel

            $p_{ki}sum = p_{ki}sum + p_{ki}$

            $\hat{\boldsymbol{\mu}}_k = \hat{\boldsymbol{\mu}}_k + (p_{ki} * \boldsymbol{x}_i)$

        $\hat{\boldsymbol{\mu}}_k = \hat{\boldsymbol{\mu}}_k/p_{ki}sum$

        $\hat{\boldsymbol{\mu}}_K = \text{append}(\hat{\boldsymbol{\mu}}_K, \hat{\boldsymbol{\mu}}_k)$

    // estimate covariance, $\hat{\Sigma}_k = \dfrac{\sum_{i=1}^{n} P(k|\boldsymbol{x}_i) * ((\boldsymbol{x}_i - \hat{\boldsymbol{\mu}}_k)^t(\boldsymbol{x}_i - \hat{\boldsymbol{\mu}}_k))}{\sum_{i=1}^{n} P(k|\boldsymbol{x}_i)}$

    $\hat{\boldsymbol{\Sigma}}_K = []$ // store covariance of K kernels

    for $k = 1$ *to* K **do**

        $\hat{\boldsymbol{\Sigma}}_k = [0\ 0;\ 0\ 0]$

        $p_{ki}sum = 0$ // sum of posteriors per k^{th} kernel

        $\hat{\boldsymbol{\mu}}_k = \hat{\boldsymbol{\mu}}_K(k)$ // mean of kth kernel

        for $i = 1$ *to* n **do**

            $\boldsymbol{x}_i = \boldsymbol{x}(i)$ // each data observation

            $p_{ki} = \text{posterior(i)(k)}$// posterior of each $\boldsymbol{x}_i$ for each kth kernel

            $p_{ki}sum = p_{ki}sum + p_{ki}$

            $\hat{\boldsymbol{\Sigma}}_k = \hat{\boldsymbol{\Sigma}}_k + p_{ki} * ((\boldsymbol{x}_i - \hat{\boldsymbol{\mu}}_k)^t * (\boldsymbol{x}_i - \hat{\boldsymbol{\mu}}_k))$

        $\hat{\boldsymbol{\Sigma}}_k = \hat{\boldsymbol{\Sigma}}_k/p_{ki}sum$

        $\hat{\boldsymbol{\Sigma}}_K = \text{append}(\hat{\boldsymbol{\Sigma}}_K, \hat{\boldsymbol{\Sigma}}_k)$

    return w_K, $\hat{\boldsymbol{\mu}}_K$, $\hat{\boldsymbol{\Sigma}}_K$

Algorithm 4.5: Pseudocode for calculation of log likelihood for EM algorithm.

Function `computeLogLikelihood`(*evidence*, *n*):

   // calculate log likelihood, $\sum_{i=1}^{n} log\left[\sum_{k=1}^{K} P(\boldsymbol{x}_i|k) * P(k)\right]$

   logLikelihood = 0

   for $i = 1\ to\ n$ **do**

      e_i = evidence(i)

      logLikelihood = logLikelihood + log(e_i)

   return *logLikelihood*

4.3   EM and KDE Validation

EM and KDE implementations were validated using a synthetic dataset. The dataset was first generated using prescribed means and covariances corresponding to six distinct Gaussian classes, with each class having an equal weight (see Table 4.1). Figure 4.1a shows the synthetic data generated using means, covariances, and weights corresponding to Gaussian classes given in Table 4.1. Each datapoint in the synthetic data was evaluated using KDE (Equations 4.1 and 4.2) with Gaussian kernels having prescribed means, covariances, and weights as shown in Table 4.1. Figure 4.1b shows $\hat{p}(\boldsymbol{x})$ estimated using KDE with Gaussian kernels corresponding to prescribed means, covariances, and weights.

Class No.	Synthetic Data Mean	Synthetic Data Covariance	Class Weight
1	[20,20]	$\begin{bmatrix} 3 & 2 \\ 2 & 3 \end{bmatrix}$	$\dfrac{1}{6}$
2	[-20,-20]	$\begin{bmatrix} 3 & -2 \\ -2 & 3 \end{bmatrix}$	$\dfrac{1}{6}$
3	[-40,-40]	$\begin{bmatrix} 5 & 0 \\ 0 & 1 \end{bmatrix}$	$\dfrac{1}{6}$
4	[10,-20]	$\begin{bmatrix} 5 & 4 \\ 4 & 6 \end{bmatrix}$	$\dfrac{1}{6}$
5	[0,0]	$\begin{bmatrix} 1 & 0 \\ 0 & 5 \end{bmatrix}$	$\dfrac{1}{6}$
6	[-10,20]	$\begin{bmatrix} 5 & -4 \\ -4 & 6 \end{bmatrix}$	$\dfrac{1}{6}$

Table 4.1: Prescribed means and covariances of six classes of Gaussian-distributed synthetic data. Each class has an equal weight.

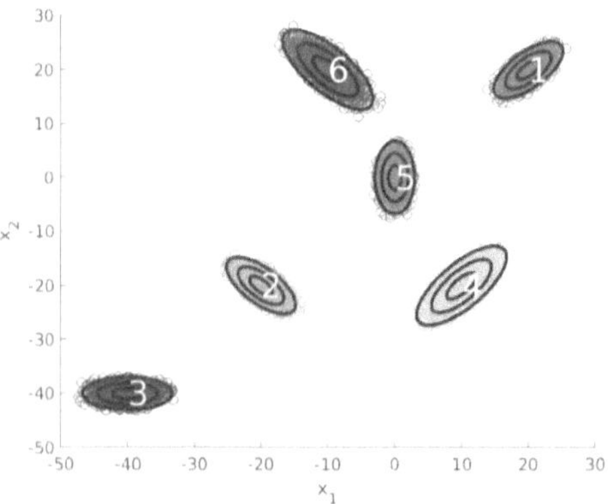

(a) Synthetic data (colored dots) generated using prescribed means, covariances, and weights from Table 4.1. The ellipses, overlaid on data, represent 1-,2-,3- standard deviations from the mean. Each class is numbered and corresponds
to Table 4.1.

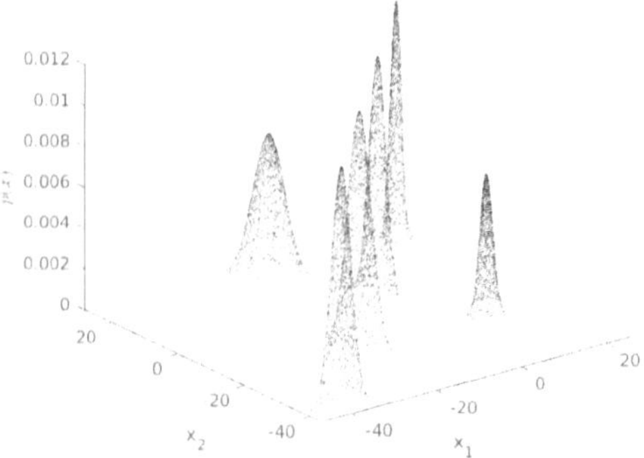

(b) $\hat{p}(\boldsymbol{x})$ estimated using KDE with six Gaussian kernels having prescribed means, covariances, and weights given in
Table 4.1.

Figure 4.1: Visualization of Gaussian-distributed synthetic data and $\hat{p}(\boldsymbol{x})$ estimated using Gaussian
kernels with prescribed means, covariances, and weights.

The EM algorithm was performed on the synthetic data with $K = 6$, as the data
contained six Gaussian classes. Table 4.2 shows the EM-estimated kernel parameters
$\hat{\boldsymbol{\mu}}$, $\hat{\boldsymbol{\Sigma}}$, and weights. Note, the estimated parameters of Gaussian kernels are similar to
the prescribed means, covariances, and weights of Gaussian classes shown in Table 4.1.
Figure 4.2a shows the synthetic data with six Gaussian classes (means, covariances,

weights from Table 4.1). However, the ellipses overlaid on synthetic data represent the Gaussian kernels estimated by EM. As the ellipses overlay the data that represents Gaussian classes, it shows that the EM algorithm finds the correct parameters for the Gaussian kernels. Furthermore, KDE was performed using the EM-estimated kernel parameters $\hat{\mu}$, $\hat{\Sigma}$, and weights. Each datapoint in the synthetic data was evaluated using KDE (Equations 4.1 and 4.2) with EM-estimated kernel parameters shown in Table 4.2. Figure 4.2b shows $\hat{p}(\boldsymbol{x})$ estimated using KDE with Gaussian kernels with EM-estimated means, covariances, and weights. Note, its similarity to Figure 4.1b, which validates the KDE implementation.

Kernel No.	$\hat{\mu}$	$\hat{\Sigma}$	Estimated Kernel Weight
1	[20,20]	$\begin{bmatrix} 2.9985 & 1.9990 \\ 1.9990 & 2.9985 \end{bmatrix}$	0.1667
2	[-20,-20]	$\begin{bmatrix} 2.9985 & -1.9990 \\ -1.9990 & 2.9985 \end{bmatrix}$	0.1667
3	[-40,-40]	$\begin{bmatrix} 4.9975 & 0.0000 \\ 0.0000 & 0.9995 \end{bmatrix}$	0.1667
4	[10,-20]	$\begin{bmatrix} 4.9975 & 3.9980 \\ 3.9980 & 5.9970 \end{bmatrix}$	0.1667
5	$1.0e^-6 * [0.0294, -0.3991]$	$\begin{bmatrix} 0.9995 & 0.0000 \\ 0.0000 & 4.9975 \end{bmatrix}$	0.1667
6	[-10,20]	$\begin{bmatrix} 4.9975 & -3.9980 \\ -3.9980 & 5.9970 \end{bmatrix}$	0.1667

Table 4.2: EM-estimated means, covariances, and weights of Gaussian kernels derived from synthetic data.

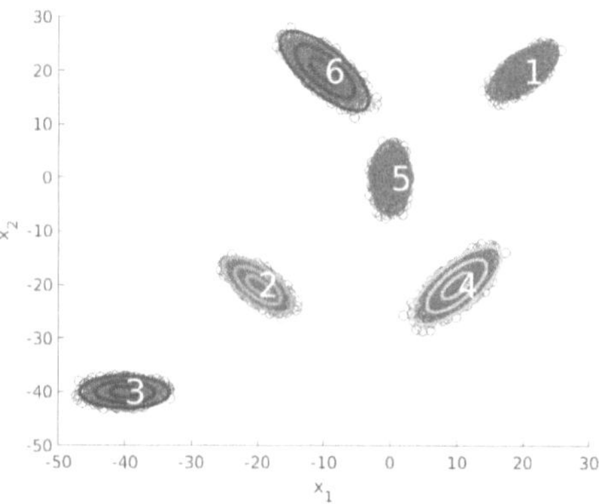

(a) The ellipses represent the Gaussian kernels estimated by EM. They overlay the six Gaussian classes comprising the synthetic dataset (blue dots). The ellipses, which represent 1-,2-,3- standard deviations from the EM-estimated mean, were computed using the EM-estimated kernel parameters. Each kernel is numbered and corresponds to Table 4.2.

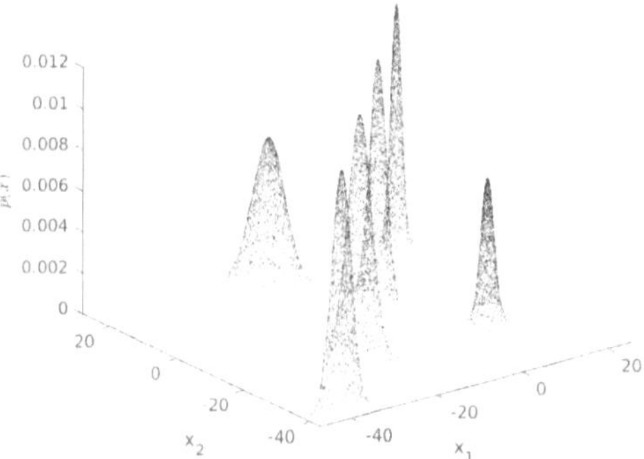

(b) $\hat{p}(\boldsymbol{x})$ estimated using the KDE with EM-estimated $\hat{\boldsymbol{\mu}}$, $\hat{\boldsymbol{\Sigma}}$, and weights.

Figure 4.2: Visualization of Gaussian kernels as found using the EM algorithm and $\hat{p}(\boldsymbol{x})$ estimated using Gaussian kernels with EM-estimated means, covariances, and weights.

4.4 Selection of KDE Kernels

To select an optimal number of K kernels, EM algorithm was used on a sample of mobile network data containing 1,000,000 observations from January 01, 2019 to January 07, 2019. As the EM algorithm proceeded, the value of K was initially set at 30. However, the algorithm produced Gaussian kernels that were *pathological*. A pathological kernel is defined as a kernel with a ratio of eigenvalues of minor and major axes to be less than 0.001. Consequently, this kernel has an extremely narrow spread across one or both data dimensions. Figure 4.3 shows two pathological kernels with ellipses representing standard deviation from the mean. As the latitude dimension is collapsed, the ellipses look like a line.

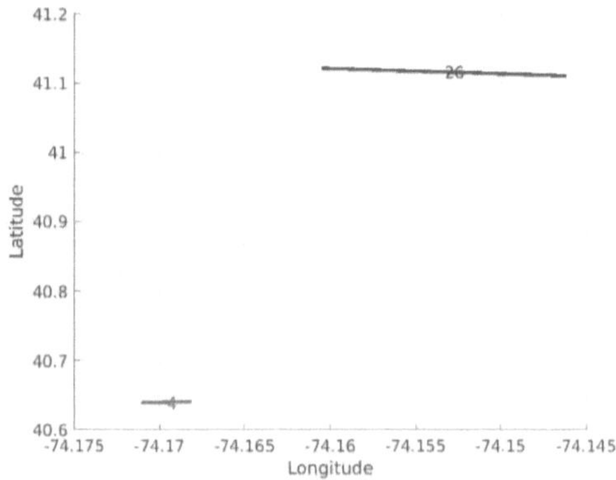

Figure 4.3: Pathological Gaussian kernels with a small standard deviation across the latitude dimension.

It is suspected that the occurrence of pathological kernels is caused by having a high number of K kernels as they are *forced* to be within tight, narrow boundaries. The EM algorithm was run iteratively with decreasing K to eliminate pathological kernels. The iterative search was stopped at $K = 22$ when the pathological kernels disappeared. Also, setting K at 22 ensured that the EM algorithm found kernels that represented user density in a realistic way. Figure 4.4 shows a scatter plot of 500,000 sample observations (i.e., latitude and longitude of mobile devices). The overlaid ellipses in the figure were computed using EM-estimated parameters with $K = 22$. The area from longitude -73.7 to -74.1 and latitude 40.6 to 41.0 shows numerous EM-found kernels that are small and at a relatively close distance. It is speculated that the area contains high user population with varying densities, i.e., a busy downtown area.

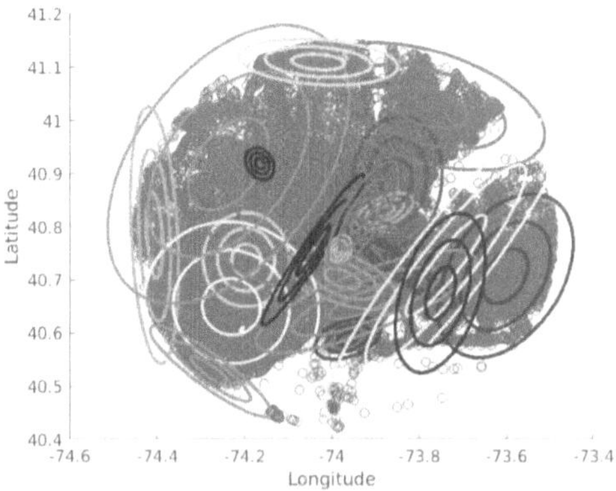

Figure 4.4: Gaussian kernels found using the EM algorithm with $K = 22$. The ellipses, which represent 1-,2-,3- standard deviations from the mean, were computed using EM-estimated parameters. The blue dots represent 500,000 sample observations (latitude and longitude of mobile devices) from August 1, 2018 to August 14, 2018.

Furthermore, KDE was performed on the above-mentioned 500,000 sample observations using EM-found Gaussian kernels with parameters $\hat{\boldsymbol{\mu}}$ and $\hat{\boldsymbol{\Sigma}}$. Figure 4.5 shows user density, $\hat{p}(\boldsymbol{x})$, estimated using KDE. The blue-yellow contours represent regions of high density along with sample observations (red dots). The selection of $K = 22$ kernels is a proper choice as it allows the KDE algorithm to find a realistic user density as evidenced by the region from longitude -73.7 to -74.1 and latitude 40.6 to 41.0. A lower number of kernels does not capture this density resolution. Note, $\hat{p}(\boldsymbol{x})$ ranges from 0-80 due to numerical instability, explained further in Section 4.5.

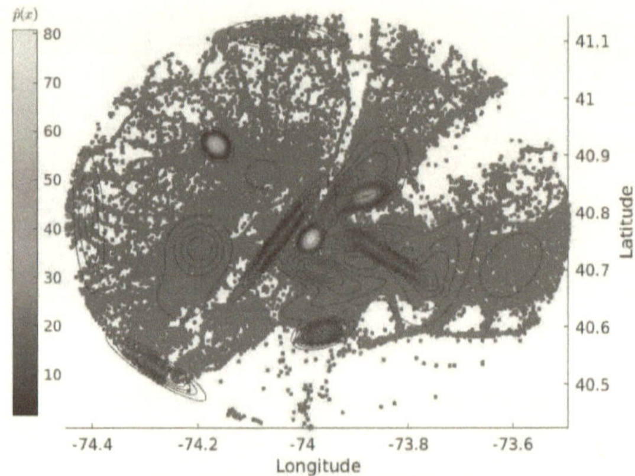

Figure 4.5: User density, $\hat{p}(\boldsymbol{x})$, estimated using KDE with EM-estimated Gaussian kernels (i.e., $K = 22$). The contours represent user densities. The red dots represent 500,000 sample observations (latitude and longitude of mobile devices) from August 1, 2018 to August 14, 2018.

Figure 4.6a shows user densities (blue regions) estimated using KDE on a geographic map (i.e., of New York city and surrounding areas). Note its similarity to Figure 4.5. Figure 4.6b shows a magnified view of one of the dense regions in New York city, the midtown Manhattan Island. Referring to Figure 4.4, this is the region that contains numerous EM-found kernels. It is a popular tourist destination comprising of iconic buildings and famous landmarks, with commerical businesses where locals come to work and shop. Hence, it is expected that a high number of mobile subscribers will be dispersed throughout this area.

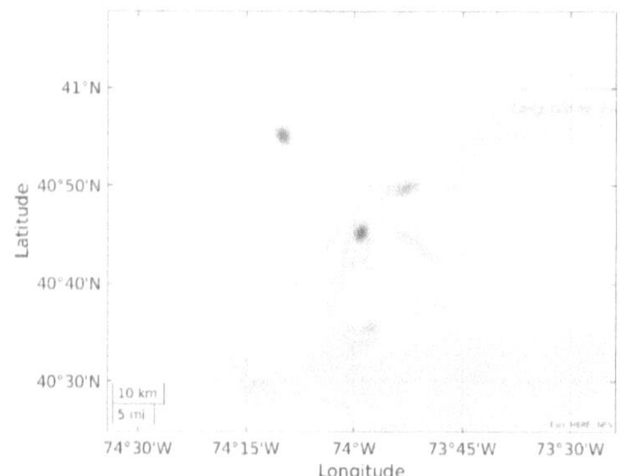

(a) User densities estimated using KDE, represented on a geographic map of New York city and surrounding areas. The blue regions show high density of mobile users on Manhattan Island, parts of New Jersey and Long Island.

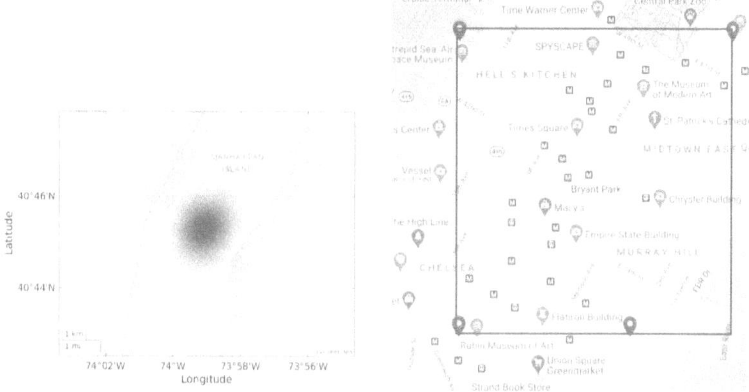

(b) A close-up view of Midtown Manhattan Island with high mobile subscriber density. The map on the right shows the famous landmarks, buildings, offices, etc where a high number of mobile users are found.

Figure 4.6: Geographic map showing mobile subscriber density estimated using KDE on 500,000 sample observations (latitude and longitude of mobile devices) from August 1, 2018 to August 14, 2018.

4.5 Numerical Instability and Data Scaling

User density estimates, $\hat{p}(\boldsymbol{x})$, shown in Figures 4.5 and 4.7, are not valid PDFs as they range from 0 to 80. The second axiom of probability states that $P(S) = 1$ (see Equation 4.4); therefore, $\hat{p}(\boldsymbol{x})$ is not a valid PDF as user density estimates are more than 1.

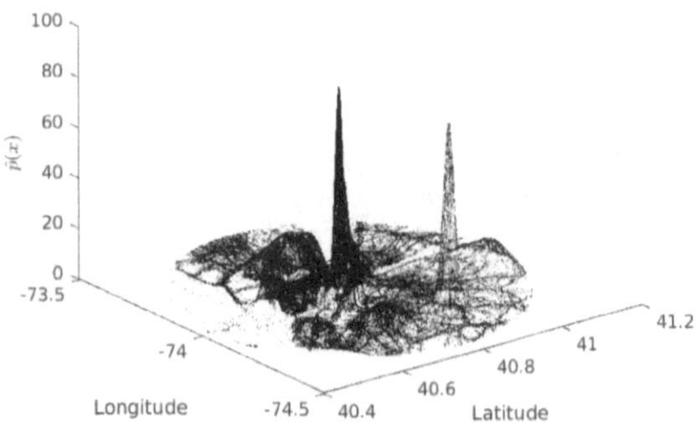

Figure 4.7: User density estimates, $\hat{p}(\boldsymbol{x})$, for 500,000 sample observations (latitude and longitude of mobile devices) from August 1, 2018 to August 14, 2018. $\hat{p}(\boldsymbol{x})$ is between 0 and 80 suggesting that it is not a valid PDF.

It is speculated that the Gaussian kernels' parameter, $\hat{\boldsymbol{\Sigma}}$, estimated by the EM algorithm causes numerical instability due to floating point representation. Tables 4.3 and 4.4 show the $\hat{\boldsymbol{\Sigma}}$ of each kernel. Note, $\hat{\boldsymbol{\Sigma}}$ is a positive definite matrix as each eigenvalue of $\hat{\boldsymbol{\Sigma}}$ is positive. Also note, the eigenvalues of $\hat{\boldsymbol{\Sigma}}$ are in the range of 10^{-6} to 10^{-3}. As Matlab stores 64-bit floating point numbers using the IEEE-754 standard, the resolution of $\hat{\boldsymbol{\Sigma}}$ causes a precision error in the estimation of $\hat{p}(\boldsymbol{x})$ when computing Equations 4.1 and 4.2. Also, the EM algorithm is iterative and the precision error is propagated when the $\hat{\boldsymbol{\Sigma}}$ is used for computations during the E and M steps (Section 4.2). The numerical instability issue was confirmed by calculating the integral of each EM-estimated kernel, shown in Tables 4.3 and 4.4. The integral of each Gaussian kernel was computed numerically using Maplesoft [3]. While performing numerical integration, the resolution of $\hat{\boldsymbol{\Sigma}}$ caused a precision error as computed results could not be respresented using the IEEE-754 standard for 64-bit floating point values. Therefore, the numerical integration gave invalid integrals (i.e., not equal to 1). It is concluded that the EM-found kernels are *not* proper Gaussians, i.e., they violate the second axiom of probability (see Equation 4.4). Consequently, $\hat{p}(\boldsymbol{x})$ estimated by the KDE is not a proper probability density function. To mitigate the issue of numerical instability, the data was scaled by a factor of 10^4 thereby producing proper integrals, i.e., equal to 1 (see Tables 4.5 and 4.6) and valid user density estimates, $\hat{p}(\boldsymbol{x})$.

Kernel No.	$\hat{\Sigma}$	1st eigenvalue	2nd eigenvalue	Integral
1	$\begin{bmatrix} 2.22*10^{-04} & 2.57*10^{-04} \\ 2.57*10^{-04} & 3.19*10^{-03} \end{bmatrix}$	$2.00*10^{-04}$	$3.21*10^{-03}$	Inf
2	$\begin{bmatrix} 6.50*10^{-03} & -3.87*10^{-04} \\ -3.87*10^{-04} & 3.33*10^{-04} \end{bmatrix}$	$3.09*10^{-04}$	$6.52*10^{-03}$	$5.86*10^{+0.}$
3	$\begin{bmatrix} 2.63*10^{-03} & 1.05*10^{-03} \\ 1.05*10^{-03} & 2.66*10^{-03} \end{bmatrix}$	$1.60*10^{-03}$	$3.70*10^{-03}$	1.02
4	$\begin{bmatrix} 8.64*10^{-04} & -3.96*10^{-06} \\ -3.96*10^{-06} & 1.08*10^{-03} \end{bmatrix}$	$8.64*10^{-04}$	$1.08*10^{-03}$	Inf
5	$\begin{bmatrix} 3.37*10^{-03} & 5.92*10^{-04} \\ 5.92*10^{-04} & 5.45*10^{-03} \end{bmatrix}$	$3.21*10^{-03}$	$5.60*10^{-03}$	$7.40*10^{-0}$
6	$\begin{bmatrix} 6.06*10^{-04} & -9.48*10^{-04} \\ -9.48*10^{-04} & 1.72*10^{-03} \end{bmatrix}$	$6.28*10^{-05}$	$2.26*10^{-03}$	$1.45*10^{-1}$
7	$\begin{bmatrix} 1.25*10^{-04} & 1.29*10^{-04} \\ 1.29*10^{-04} & 4.56*10^{-04} \end{bmatrix}$	$8.08*10^{-05}$	$5.00*10^{-04}$	$1.74*10^{+2}$
8	$\begin{bmatrix} 1.67*10^{-03} & 1.34*10^{-04} \\ 1.34*10^{-04} & 1.20*10^{-03} \end{bmatrix}$	$1.16*10^{-03}$	$1.71*10^{-03}$	1.06
9	$\begin{bmatrix} 3.62*10^{-04} & -4.12*10^{-04} \\ -4.12*10^{-04} & 1.63*10^{-03} \end{bmatrix}$	$2.41*10^{-04}$	$1.76*10^{-03}$	$4.61*10^{-2}$
10	$\begin{bmatrix} 2.85*10^{-03} & -1.67*10^{-04} \\ -1.67*10^{-04} & 4.46*10^{-03} \end{bmatrix}$	$2.83*10^{-03}$	$4.48*10^{-03}$	$1.44*10^{+0}$
11	$\begin{bmatrix} 1.67*10^{-04} & 1.35*10^{-04} \\ 1.35*10^{-04} & 6.32*10^{-04} \end{bmatrix}$	$1.30*10^{-04}$	$6.68*10^{-04}$	$4.90*10^{-2}$

Table 4.3: Integrals of EM-found kernels as calculated using Maplesoft [3], using 500,000 sample observations (latitude and longitude of mobile devices) from August 1, 2018 to August 14, 2018.

Kernel No.	$\hat{\Sigma}$	1st eigenvalue	2nd eigenvalue	Integral
12	$\begin{bmatrix} 1.04 * 10^{-03} & 2.10 * 10^{-03} \\ 2.10 * 10^{-03} & 7.04 * 10^{-03} \end{bmatrix}$	$3.73 * 10^{-04}$	$7.70 * 10^{-03}$	$8.79 * 10^{-16}$
13	$\begin{bmatrix} 1.59 * 10^{-03} & -1.56 * 10^{-03} \\ -1.56 * 10^{-03} & 8.06 * 10^{-03} \end{bmatrix}$	$1.23 * 10^{-03}$	$8.41 * 10^{-03}$	$5.04 * 10^{-01}$
14	$\begin{bmatrix} 2.22 * 10^{-03} & 1.77 * 10^{-03} \\ 1.77 * 10^{-03} & 1.51 * 10^{-03} \end{bmatrix}$	$5.77 * 10^{-05}$	$3.67 * 10^{-03}$	$5.30 * 10^{+278}$
15	$\begin{bmatrix} 8.95 * 10^{-03} & 7.98 * 10^{-03} \\ 7.98 * 10^{-03} & 8.43 * 10^{-03} \end{bmatrix}$	$7.02 * 10^{-04}$	$1.67 * 10^{-02}$	8.33
16	$\begin{bmatrix} 8.03 * 10^{-04} & -1.18 * 10^{-03} \\ -1.18 * 10^{-03} & 2.14 * 10^{-03} \end{bmatrix}$	$1.16 * 10^{-04}$	$2.83 * 10^{-03}$	$1.29 * 10^{+59}$
17	$\begin{bmatrix} 7.56 * 10^{-03} & 3.73 * 10^{-03} \\ 3.73 * 10^{-03} & 8.50 * 10^{-03} \end{bmatrix}$	$4.27 * 10^{-03}$	$1.18 * 10^{-02}$	1.04
18	$\begin{bmatrix} 1.00 * 10^{-04} & 3.18 * 10^{-05} \\ 3.18 * 10^{-05} & 9.29 * 10^{-05} \end{bmatrix}$	$6.46 * 10^{-05}$	$1.29 * 10^{-04}$	$3.64 * 10^{+217}$
19	$\begin{bmatrix} 1.08 * 10^{-03} & 6.95 * 10^{-04} \\ 6.95 * 10^{-04} & 7.34 * 10^{-04} \end{bmatrix}$	$1.92 * 10^{-04}$	$1.63 * 10^{-03}$	$1.55 * 10^{-03}$
20	$\begin{bmatrix} 2.06 * 10^{-04} & -1.87 * 10^{-04} \\ -1.87 * 10^{-04} & 3.65 * 10^{-03} \end{bmatrix}$	$1.96 * 10^{-04}$	$3.66 * 10^{-03}$	Inf
21	$\begin{bmatrix} 1.00 * 10^{-04} & -2.66 * 10^{-05} \\ -2.66 * 10^{-05} & 1.19 * 10^{-04} \end{bmatrix}$	$8.16 * 10^{-05}$	$1.38 * 10^{-04}$	$3.02 * 10^{+57}$
22	$\begin{bmatrix} 2.49 * 10^{-03} & 7.30 * 10^{-04} \\ 7.30 * 10^{-04} & 1.18 * 10^{-03} \end{bmatrix}$	$8.53 * 10^{-04}$	$2.82 * 10^{-03}$	$1.38 * 10^{+01}$

Table 4.4: Integrals of EM-found kernels as calculated using Maplesoft [3], using 500,000 sample observations (latitude and longitude of mobile devices) from August 1, 2018 to August 14, 2018.

Kernel No.	$\hat{\Sigma}$	1st eigenvalue	2nd eigenvalue	Integral
1	$\begin{bmatrix} 2.22 * 10^{+04} & 2.57 * 10^{+04} \\ 2.57 * 10^{+04} & 3.19 * 10^{+05} \end{bmatrix}$	$2.00 * 10^{+04}$	$3.21 * 10^{+05}$	1.00
2	$\begin{bmatrix} 6.50 * 10^{+05} & -3.87 * 10^{+04} \\ -3.87 * 10^{+04} & 3.33 * 10^{+04} \end{bmatrix}$	$3.09 * 10^{+04}$	$6.52 * 10^{+05}$	1.00
3	$\begin{bmatrix} 2.63 * 10^{+05} & 1.05 * 10^{+05} \\ 1.05 * 10^{+05} & 2.66 * 10^{+05} \end{bmatrix}$	$1.60 * 10^{+05}$	$3.70 * 10^{+05}$	1.00
4	$\begin{bmatrix} 8.64 * 10^{+04} & -3.96 * 10^{+02} \\ -3.96 * 10^{+02} & 1.08 * 10^{+05} \end{bmatrix}$	$8.64 * 10^{+04}$	$1.08 * 10^{+05}$	1.00
5	$\begin{bmatrix} 3.37 * 10^{+05} & 5.92 * 10^{+04} \\ 5.92 * 10^{+04} & 5.45 * 10^{+05} \end{bmatrix}$	$3.21 * 10^{+05}$	$5.60 * 10^{+05}$	1.00
6	$\begin{bmatrix} 6.06 * 10^{+04} & -9.48 * 10^{+04} \\ -9.48 * 10^{+04} & 1.72 * 10^{+05} \end{bmatrix}$	$6.28 * 10^{+03}$	$2.26 * 10^{+05}$	1.00
7	$\begin{bmatrix} 1.25 * 10^{+04} & 1.29 * 10^{+04} \\ 1.29 * 10^{+04} & 4.56 * 10^{+04} \end{bmatrix}$	$8.08 * 10^{+03}$	$5.00 * 10^{+04}$	1.00
8	$\begin{bmatrix} 1.67 * 10^{+05} & 1.34 * 10^{+04} \\ 1.34 * 10^{+04} & 1.20 * 10^{+05} \end{bmatrix}$	$1.16 * 10^{+05}$	$1.71 * 10^{+05}$	1.00
9	$\begin{bmatrix} 3.62 * 10^{+04} & -4.12 * 10^{+04} \\ -4.12 * 10^{+04} & 1.63 * 10^{+05} \end{bmatrix}$	$2.41 * 10^{+04}$	$1.76 * 10^{+05}$	1.00
10	$\begin{bmatrix} 2.85 * 10^{+05} & -1.67 * 10^{+04} \\ -1.67 * 10^{+04} & 4.46 * 10^{+05} \end{bmatrix}$	$2.83 * 10^{+05}$	$4.48 * 10^{+05}$	1.00
11	$\begin{bmatrix} 1.67 * 10^{+04} & 1.35 * 10^{+04} \\ 1.35 * 10^{+04} & 6.32 * 10^{+04} \end{bmatrix}$	$1.30 * 10^{+04}$	$6.68 * 10^{+04}$	1.00

Table 4.5: Integrals of EM-found kernels as calculated using Maplesoft [3], using 500,000 sample observations (latitude and longitude of mobile devices) from August 1, 2018 to August 14, 2018. The sample observations were scaled by a factor of 10^4.

Kernel No.	$\hat{\Sigma}$	1st eigenvalue	2nd eigenvalue	Integral
12	$\begin{bmatrix} 1.04*10^{+05} & 2.10*10^{+05} \\ 2.10*10^{+05} & 7.04*10^{+05} \end{bmatrix}$	$3.73*10^{+04}$	$7.70*10^{+05}$	1.00
13	$\begin{bmatrix} 1.59*10^{+05} & -1.56*10^{+05} \\ -1.56*10^{+05} & 8.06*10^{+05} \end{bmatrix}$	$1.23*10^{+05}$	$8.41*10^{+05}$	1.00
14	$\begin{bmatrix} 2.22*10^{+05} & 1.77*10^{+05} \\ 1.77*10^{+05} & 1.51*10^{+05} \end{bmatrix}$	$5.77*10^{+03}$	$3.67*10^{+05}$	1.00
15	$\begin{bmatrix} 8.95*10^{+05} & 7.98*10^{+05} \\ 7.98*10^{+05} & 8.43*10^{+05} \end{bmatrix}$	$7.02*10^{+04}$	$1.67*10^{+06}$	1.00
16	$\begin{bmatrix} 8.03*10^{+04} & -1.18*10^{+05} \\ -1.18*10^{+05} & 2.14*10^{+05} \end{bmatrix}$	$1.16*10^{+04}$	$2.83*10^{+05}$	1.00
17	$\begin{bmatrix} 7.56*10^{+05} & 3.73*10^{+05} \\ 3.73*10^{+05} & 8.50*10^{+05} \end{bmatrix}$	$4.27*10^{+05}$	$1.18*10^{+06}$	1.00
18	$\begin{bmatrix} 1.00*10^{+04} & 3.18*10^{+03} \\ 3.18*10^{+03} & 9.29*10^{+03} \end{bmatrix}$	$6.46*10^{+03}$	$1.29*10^{+04}$	1.00
19	$\begin{bmatrix} 1.08*10^{+05} & 6.95*10^{+04} \\ 6.95*10^{+04} & 7.34*10^{+04} \end{bmatrix}$	$1.92*10^{+04}$	$1.63*10^{+05}$	1.00
20	$\begin{bmatrix} 2.06*10^{+04} & -1.87*10^{+04} \\ -1.87*10^{+04} & 3.65*10^{+05} \end{bmatrix}$	$1.96*10^{+04}$	$3.66*10^{+05}$	1.00
21	$\begin{bmatrix} 1.00*10^{+04} & -2.66*10^{+03} \\ -2.66*10^{+03} & 1.19*10^{+04} \end{bmatrix}$	$8.16*10^{+03}$	$1.38*10^{+04}$	1.00
22	$\begin{bmatrix} 2.49*10^{+05} & 7.30*10^{+04} \\ 7.30*10^{+04} & 1.18*10^{+05} \end{bmatrix}$	$8.53*10^{+04}$	$2.82*10^{+05}$	1.00

Table 4.6: Integrals of EM-found kernels as calculated using Maplesoft [3], using 500,000 sample observations (latitude and longitude of mobile devices) from August 1, 2018 to August 14, 2018. The sample observations were scaled by a factor of 10^4.

4.6   Chapter Summary

Kernel Density Estimation and Expectation Maximization were used to estimate user densities in a large urban area from the mobile network data. Both KDE and EM algorithms were verified using a synthetic dataset consisting of six distinct classes of Gaussian-distributed data. The choice of K kernels for the EM algorithm was based on an iterative search. The EM algorithm was run with varying K until the pathological clusters disappeared at $K = 22$.

The issue of numerical instability surfaced due to the resolution of EM-estimated kernels' parameter $\hat{\Sigma}$. This caused a precision error when i) estimating user densities, $\hat{p}(\boldsymbol{x})$, using KDE and ii) iteratively running E and M steps of the EM algorithm to estimate $\hat{\Sigma}$. The data was scaled by a factor of 10^4 to ensure that the EM algorithm found proper Gaussian kernels (i.e., met probability axioms). Also, scaling of data ensured that valid user densities, $\hat{p}(\boldsymbol{x})$, were estimated by KDE.

Chapter 5

Analysis of User Density and Quality of Service

Based on the user density model, as obtained from the Kernel Density Estimation (KDE) and Expectation Maximization (EM) from Chapter 4, the available data was further analyzed to determine:

1. Variability in User Densities: Biweekly periods of data were statistically analyzed to determine their rate of change over time, i.e., over what period statistical stationarity can be reasonably assumed to hold.

2. How user density impacts QoS: The QoS behaviours for areas defined to be of low, medium, and high user densities were statistically compared.

5.1 Statistical Analysis of User Distribution

The Anderson-Darling test is a goodness-of-fit statistical test. Suppose there are K samples, with $k = 1, ..., K$, and each sample has a continuous distribution F_k. The AD test has the following null hypothesis [83]:

$$H_0:\ F_1 = F_2\ ... = F_K$$

and the following alternative hypothesis:

$$H_a:\ F_1 \neq F_2\ ... \neq F_K$$

If the null hypothesis holds, then the K samples have a common continuous distribution F [83]. Note, the AD test determines if the K samples come from F without specifying the distribution itself [83]. Each *sample* corresponds to data from a biweekly period as described in Table 3.2. The following explains the reasons for choosing K-sample Anderson-Darling test for the statistical analysis of user density distribution:

1. The test takes into account variable sample sizes.

2. The test is sensitive to the changes in the overall shape of the user density distribution.

5.1.1 Anderson-Darling Test Procedure

The Anderson-Darling test is a one-dimensional, distribution-free test [83]. The AD test uses the notion of a *pooled* sample, which combines multiple K samples. Each k sample consists of N_k observations. Let $N = \sum_{k=1}^{K} N_k$ be the number of observations in the pooled sample and let $Z_1^* < ... < Z_L^*$ denote L distinct, ordered observations in the pooled sample. Furthermore, let f_{kj} be the number of observations in the kth sample coinciding with Z_j^* and let $l_j = \sum_{k=1}^{K} f_{kj}$ be the number of observations in all K samples coinciding with Z_j^*. Then the AD test statistic is [83]:

$$A_{KN}^2 = \sum_{k=1}^{K} \frac{1}{N_k} \sum_{j=1}^{L-1} \frac{l_j}{N} \frac{(NM_{kj} - N_k B_j)^2}{B_j(N - B_j)} \tag{5.1}$$

where $M_{kj} = f_{k1} + ... + f_{kj}$ and $B_j = l_1 + ... + l_j$. As the mobile network data is two-dimensional, the AD test was conducted on each dimension separately. Furthermore, ties exist in the data as it is discrete, where a tie is defined as observations having the *same* value. Equation 5.1 handles data with tied observations. The AD test statistic has a probability distribution with mean (Equation 5.2) and variance (Equation 5.3). Higher moments of A_{KN}^2 are difficult to compute, as noted by Scholz and Stephens [83].

$$\mu_N = mean(A_{KN}^2) = K - 1 \tag{5.2}$$

$$\sigma_N^2 = var(A_{KN}^2) = \frac{aN^3 + bN^2 + cN + d}{(N-1)(N-2)(N-3)} \tag{5.3}$$

with

$$a = (4g - 6)(K - 1) + (10 - 6g)H$$
$$b = (2g - 4)K^2 + 8hK + (2g - 14h - 4)H - 8h + 4g - 6$$

$$c = (6h + 2g - 2)K^2 + (4h - 4g + 6)K + (2h - 6)H + 4h$$
$$d = (2h + 6)K^2 - 4hK$$

where

$$H = \sum_{k=1}^{K} \frac{1}{N_k} \qquad h = \sum_{i=1}^{N-1} \frac{1}{i}$$

and

$$g = \sum_{i=1}^{N-2} \sum_{t=i+1}^{N-1} \frac{1}{(N-i)t}$$

$$T_{KN}^{norm} = \frac{|A_{KN}^2 - \mu_N|}{\sqrt{\sigma_N^2}} \tag{5.4}$$

The normalized AD test statistic (Equation 5.4) has T^{norm} distribution, as described by authors of [83], with critical values shown in Table 5.1 at α significance level. The normalized AD test statistic is used in conjunction with Table 5.1 when applying the AD test procedure. Algorithm 5.1 shows the steps for the AD test procedure.

	α		
μ_N	.25	0.05	0.01
1	0.326	1.960	3.752
2	0.449	1.945	3.414
3	0.498	1.915	3.246
4	0.525	1.894	3.139

Table 5.1: Critical values for T^{norm} distribution.

Algorithm 5.1: AD test procedure.

Step 1: Calculate the AD test statistic, A^2_{KN}, with Equation 5.1.

Step 2: Calculate the mean of AD test statistic, μ_N, with Equation 5.2.

Step 3: Calculate the variance of AD test statistic, σ^2_N, with Equation 5.3.

Step 4: Calculate the normalized AD test statistic, T^{norm}_{KN}, with Equation 5.4.

Step 5: Use T^{norm}_{KN} with Table 5.1 to determine if the null hypothesis holds. Compare T^{norm}_{KN} with critical value of T^{norm} distribution at μ_N and α.

Step 6:

if $T^{norm}_{KN} > T^{norm}$ *at* μ_N *and* α **then**
| Reject H_0
else
| Fail to reject H_0
end

5.1.2 Anderson-Darling Test Implementation and Validation

Due to the orientation of Manhattan Island, there is a correlation between the latitude and longitude coordinates of user device locations. As the AD test was conducted on each data dimension separately, the data was orthogonalized to remove the correlation between latitude and longitude. An average of eigenvectors was computed using correlation matrices from data samples' latitude and longitude. The data samples were then projected onto the average eigenvector and the AD test was performed on each decorrelated sample dimension. Algorithm 5.2 shows the pseudocode for average eigenvector computation. $E1$ corresponds to a set of eigenvectors related to the major axis of each data sample. Similarly, $E2$ corresponds to a set of eigenvectors related to the minor axis of each data sample. Taking an average of $E1$, $E2$ gives a pair of $e1$, $e2$ eigenvectors for the orthogonalization of data samples. Note, normalizing $e1$, $e2$ ensures that the eigenvectors are unit vectors.

Algorithm 5.2: Pseudocode for average eigenvector.

```
// @dirPath:  path to dir containing samples
Function AvgEigVec(dirPath):
    E1 = [] // set of e1 eigenvectors (major axis)
    E2 = [] // set of e2 eigenvectors (minor axis)
    for k = 1 to length(dirPath) do
        // load each dataset
        data = load(dirPath(k))
        // decompose covariance of k^th data sample
        [eigVec, eigVal] = eig(cov(data))
        // sort eigenvalues from highest to lowest variance
        [eigVal, idx] = sort(eigVal, 'descend')
        // get eigenvectors based on sorted eigenvalues
        eigVec = eigVec(:, idx)
        // collect E1 and E2
        E1 = append(E1, eigVec(:,1)) // (e1_1, e1_2, e1_3, ...)
        E2 = append(E2, eigVec(:,2)) // (e2_1, e2_2, e2_3, ...)
    // average of E1, column vector
    e1 = mean(E1,2)
    // normalize e1 so it is unit vector
    len_e1 = sqrt(e1(1)^2 + e1(2)^2) // magnitude of e1
    e1 = e1/len_e1 // divide the vector by magnitude of e1
    //
    // similarly, get average of E2 as e2 and normalize
    //
    // verify that e1, e2 are orthogonal
    assert(dot(e1, e2) == 0)
    // store the eigenvectors (e1, e2)
    e = [e1 e2]
    return e
```

Algorithm 5.3: Pseudocode for K-sample Anderson-Darling test statistic.

```
// @K: number of samples
```

```
// @samples: all K samples combined
```

```
// @recNum: keeps track of observations belonging to k^th sample
```

```
// @N: total observations in pooled sample
```

```
// @lstN_k: list of sample sizes
```

Function ADTestStatistic(*samples, recNum, K, N, lstN_k*):

   // unique observations in pooled sample, sorted ascending

   $Z = \mathrm{unique}(\mathrm{sort}(\mathrm{samples}))$

   $L = \mathrm{length}(Z)$ // total number of unique observations in pooled sample

   $A^2_{KN} = 0$ // AD test statistic

   // traverse K samples

   for $k = 1\ to\ K$ **do**

      $sample_k = \mathrm{samples}(\mathrm{recNum} == k)$ // k^{th} sample

      $N_k = lstN_k(k)$ // num of observations in k^{th} sample

      $M_{kj} = 0$

      $B_j = 0$

      $AD_j = 0$

      // traverse Z

      for $j = 1\ to\ (L\text{-}1)$ **do**

         if *(Z(j) == sample_k)* **then**

            // count freq of values in k^{th} sample equal to j^{th} value in Z

            $f_{kj} = \mathrm{count}(Z(j) == sample_k)$

            $M_{kj} = M_{kj} + f_{kj}$

         /* count freq of values in the pooled sample equal to j^{th} value in Z */

         $l_j = \mathrm{count}(Z(j) == \mathrm{samples})$

         $B_j = B_j + l_j$

         // calculate the inner summation

         $\mathrm{numer} = l_j * ((N * M_{kj}) - (N_k * B_j))^2$

         $\mathrm{denom} = N * B_j * (N - B_j)$

         $AD_j = AD_j + (\mathrm{numer}\ /\ \mathrm{denom})$ // inner summation

      // calculate the outer summation

      $AD_k = AD_j * (1/N_k)$

      $A^2_{KN} = A^2_{KN} + AD_k$ // outer summation

   return A^2_{KN}

Algorithm 5.4: Pseudocode for mean and variance of AD test statistic.
Pseudocode for normalized AD test statistic.

```
// @K: number of samples
Function ADTestMean(K):
    μ_N = K-1 // mean of AD test statistic
    return μ_N
//
// @N: number of observations in pooled sample
// @K: number of samples
// @lstN_k: list of sample sizes
Function ADTestVariance(N, K, lstN_k):
    H = 0
    for k = 1 to K do
        N_k = lstN_k(k)
        H = H + (1/N_k)
    h = 0
    for i = to N-1 do
        h = h + (1/i)
    g = 0
    for i = 1 to N-2 do
        for t = i+1 to N-1 do
            g = g + 1/((N-i) * t)
    // calculate variance
    a=0; b=0; c=0; d=0
    a = (4*g-6)*(K-1)+(10-6*g)*H
    b = (2*g-4)*K^2 + 8*h*K + (2*g-14*h-4)*H - 8*h + 4*g-6
    c = (6*h+2*g-2)*K^2 + (4*h-4*g+6)*K + (2*h-6)*H + 4*h
    d = (2*h+6)*K^2 - 4*h*K
    σ_N^2 = ((a * N^3) + (b * N^2) + (c * N) + d)/((N-1) * (N-2) * (N-3))
    return σ_N^2
//
// @μ_N: mean of AD test statistic
// @σ_N^2: variance of AD test statistic
// @A_{KN}^2: AD test statistic
Function NormalizedADTest(μ_N, σ_N^2, A_{KN}^2):
    T_{KN}^{norm} = abs(A_{KN}^2 - μ_N)/ sqrt(σ_N^2)
    return T_{KN}^{norm}
```

Algorithm 5.5: Pseudocode showing steps for conducting Anderson-Darling test.

```
// @fileLst:  file paths for samples
// @avgEig:   average eigenvector to orthogonalize the samples
```

Function ConductADTest($fileLst$, $avgEig$)**:**

$samples_K = []$ // contains all pooled K samples

recNum $= []$ // keeps track of observations belonging to k^{th} sample

$lstN_k = []$ // list of sample size for each kth sample

K $= 0$ // num of samples

recVal $= 0$

// traverse files

for *file in fileLst* **do**

    sample $=$ load(file) // load k^{th} sample

    $lstN_k =$ append($lstN_k$, length(sample)) // append sample sizes

    sample $=$ sample * avgEig // orthogonalize the sample

    $samples_K =$ append($samples_K$, sample) // pool the samples

    K $=$ K $+ 1$

    // track observations for K samples

    // i.e., 1's for first sample, 2's for second sample , etc.

    recNum $=$ append(recNum, recVal * ones(:,1))

    recVal $=$ recVal $+ 1$

N $=$ length($samples_K$) // number of observations in pooled sample

// separate each dimension

$samples_K x = samples_K(:,1)$

$samples_K y = samples_K(:,2)$

// calculate AD test statistic

$A^2_{KN}x =$ ADTestStatistic($samples_K x$, recNum, K, N, $lstN_k$)

$A^2_{KN}y =$ ADTestStatistic($samples_K y$, recNum, K, N, $lstN_k$)

// calculate mean of AD test statistic

$\mu_N =$ ADTestMean(K)

// calculate variance of AD test statistic

$\sigma^2_N =$ ADTestVariance(N, K, $lstN_k$)

// calculate normalized AD test statistic

$T^{norm}_{KN}x =$ NormalizedADTest(μ_N, σ^2_N, $A^2_{KN}x$)

$T^{norm}_{KN}y =$ NormalizedADTest(μ_N, σ^2_N, $A^2_{KN}y$)

Algorithm 5.6: Pseudocode of main function for K-sample Anderson-Darling test. Top half of the main function shows the AD test conducted on data shards within a biweekly period. Bottom half of the main function shows the AD test conducted on datasets for a sequence of biweekly periods.

Function Main():

```
// get average eigenvector
dirPath = "dir containing samples" // see Table 3.2"
avgEig = AvgEigVec(dirPath) // get average eigenvector
// Perform AD test on data shards
// Example of data shards from oct1-14
// K represents number of samples, where each sample is a shard
// AD test for data shards has K ≥ 2
dirPathOct1-14 = "path for data shards from oct1-14"
fileLst = [] // contains list of file paths
// traverse data shards
for i = 1 to length(dirPathOct1-14) do
    fileLst = append(fileLst, dirPathOct1-14(i)) // append file paths
ConductADTest(fileLst, avgEig)
// Repeat the AD test for oct15-31, nov1-14, nov15-30, dec1-14, dec15-31
// Then perform AD test on a sequence of biweekly periods
// if biweekly data is sharded, then a single representative shard
   represents that period
// AD test for sequence of biweekly data has K = 2
dirPathBiweekly = "path to biweekly dataset, with a single shard
  represented for sharded data"
// traverse a pair of consecutive data samples
for curr = 1 to (length(dirPathbiweekly) - 1) do
    nxt = curr + 1
    // file path from current period and next period
    fileLst = [dirPathbiweekly(curr), dirPathbiweekly(nxt)] // filepaths
    ConductADTest(fileLst, avgEig)
```

Algorithm 5.6 shows the main function for performing the K-sample Anderson-Darling test. The pseudocode highlights the two ways the AD test was applied in the analyses, namely:

1. Test data shards within a biweekly period, i.e., test Shard no. 1, Shard no. 2, Shard no. 3, etc., to determine if they have a *common* user density distribution. If they do, then any single data shard represents user density for that particular biweekly period.

2. Test data for a pair of consecutive biweekly periods, i.e., test period 1 and period 2, test period 2 and period 3, etc. to determine if user densities are stationary over time.

The main function calls ConductADTest(), pseudocode shown in Algorithm 5.5. ConductADTest() loads the kth sample and performs orthogonalization using the average eigenvector ($e1$, $e2$). Also, it pools multiple K samples, separates the two-dimensional *pooled* data, and calls ADTestStatistic() using each separate data dimension (Algorithm 5.3). Furthermore, it gets mean and variance of AD test statistic by calling ADTestMean() and ADTestVariance() shown in Algorithm 5.4. Finally, it gets normalized AD test statistic with NormalizedADTest() shown in Algorithm 5.4. The AD test implementation was validated using sample dataset with corresponding results provided by Scholz and Stephens [83].

5.1.3 Anderson-Darling Test Results

As mentioned in Section 3.1, the data from the biweekly periods between October 15, 2018, to December 31, 2018, is divided into multiple shards. The AD test was first conducted on sharded data within each biweekly period from October 15th onward. The results for the first dimension of data are shown in Table 5.2 and second dimension in Table 5.3. The number of K samples in each row coincides with the number of data shards in each biweekly period. Based on the results, the data shards for both data dimensions within a biweekly period such as Oct 15-31, Nov 15-30, Dec 1-14, and Dec 15-31 have a similar user density distribution as the null hypothesis holds. However, for the biweekly period of Nov 1-14, the results for the first data dimension show that the data shards have different user density distributions as the null hypothesis does not hold. Note, for the biweekly period of Nov 1-14, the data shards for the second data dimension have a similar user density distribution.

Biweekly Periods containing data shards Year: 2018	K	AD^2_{KN}	T^{norm}_{KN}	T^{norm} with $\alpha = 0.05$ $\mu_N = K\text{-}1$	Reject H_0
Oct 15 - Oct 31	2	0.3082	0.9086	1.960	No
Nov 1 - Nov 14	3	5.2561	3.0239	1.945	Yes
Nov 15 - Nov 30	4	3.0246	0.0186	1.915	No
Dec 1 - Dec 14	4	2.4410	0.4238	1.915	No
Dec 15 - Dec 31	4	1.5141	1.1266	1.915	No

Table 5.2: AD test results for sharded data for each biweekly period. The results pertain to first dimension of sharded data. The number of K samples in each row coincides with the number of data shards in each biweekly period. T^{norm} comes from Table 5.1 with α=0.05 and $\mu_N = K - 1$.

Biweekly Periods containing data shards Year: 2018	K	AD^2_{KN}	T^{norm}_{KN}	T^{norm} with $\alpha = 0.05$ $\mu_N = K\text{-}1$	Reject H_0
Oct 15 - Oct 31	2	0.3904	0.8005	1.960	No
Nov 1 - Nov 14	3	1.0398	0.8917	1.945	No
Nov 15 - Nov 30	4	4.6490	1.2503	1.915	No
Dec 1 - Dec 14	4	2.2512	0.5677	1.915	No
Dec 15 - Dec 31	4	2.1299	0.6597	1.915	No

Table 5.3: AD test results for sharded data for each biweekly period. The results pertain to second dimension of sharded data. The number of K samples in each row coincides with the number of data shards in each biweekly period. T^{norm} comes from Table 5.1 with α=0.05 and $\mu_N = K - 1$.

The AD test was further conducted on data (i.e., first dimension) from biweekly period of Nov 1-14 to investigate if a majority of data shards have a similar user density distribution. Note, the AD test was performed on a pair of data shards with the number of samples $K = 2$. The results (Table 5.4) show that Shard no. 1 and Shard no. 2 have a similar user density distribution as the null hypothesis holds. Based on the results shown in Tables 5.2, 5.3, and 5.4, Shard no. 1 was selected as the representative sample for each biweekly period from October 15th onward.

Pair of Data shards from Nov1-Nov14, 2018	K	AD^2_{KN}	T^{norm}_{KN}	T^{norm} with $\alpha = 0.05$ $\mu_N = 1$	Reject H_0
Shard no. 1 and 2	2	0.7998	0.2629	1.960	No
Shard no. 2 and 3	2	4.4970	4.5929	1.960	Yes
Shard no. 1 and 3	2	2.7903	2.3514	1.960	Yes

Table 5.4: AD test results for a pair of sharded data for the period of November 1, 2018 to November 14, 2018. The results pertain to first dimension of sharded data. T^{norm} comes from Table 5.1 with α=0.05 and $\mu_N = 1$.

Finally, the AD test was conducted on data from a pair of consecutive biweekly periods from August 1, 2018, to December 31, 2018. The results for the first dimension of data are shown in Table 5.5 and second dimension in Table 5.6. Each row corresponds to a pair of samples where Sample1 is from one biweekly period and Sample2 is from the next biweekly period. Based on the results, the null hypothesis does not hold for each pair of biweekly periods; the high T^{norm}_{KN} values suggest that the samples are extreme outliers. The results conclude that the user densities are non-stationary and significantly differ from one biweekly period to the next.

Samples from a pair of consecutive Biweekly Periods Year: 2018	AD^2_{KN}	T^{norm}_{KN}	T^{norm} with $\alpha = 0.05$ $\mu_N = 1$	Reject H_0
Sample1 from Aug 1 - Aug 14 Sample2 from Aug 15 - Aug 31	1379.01	1809.83	1.960	Yes
Sample1 from Aug 15 - Aug 31 Sample2 from Sept 1 - Sept 14	4330.03	5685.59	1.960	Yes
Sample1 from Sept 1 - Sept 14 Sample2 from Sept 15 - Sept 30	2521.30	3310.07	1.960	Yes
Sample1 from Sept 15 - Sept 30 Sample2 from Oct 1 - Oct 14	6167.95	8099.45	1.960	Yes
Sample1 from Oct 1 - Oct 14 Sample2 from Oct 15 - Oct 31	749.56	983.13	1.960	Yes
Sample1 from Oct 15 - Oct 31 Sample2 from Nov 1 - Nov 14	26467.89	34760.63	1.960	Yes
Sample1 from Nov 1 - Nov 14 Sample2 from Nov 15 - Nov 30	44024.13	57818.36	1.960	Yes
Sample1 from Nov 15 - Nov 30 Sample2 from Dec 1 - Dec 14	16982.29	22302.61	1.960	Yes
Sample1 from Dec 1 - Dec 14 Sample2 Dec 15 - Dec 31	11462.27	15052.81	1.960	Yes

Table 5.5: Results for K-sample AD test with $K = 2$ for a sequence of biweekly periods. The results pertain to the first dimension of each sample. T^{norm} comes from Table 5.1 with α=0.05 and $\mu_N = 1$.

Samples from a pair of consecutive Biweekly Periods Year: 2018	AD^2_{KN}	T^{norm}_{KN}	T^{norm} with $\alpha = 0.05$ $\mu_N = 1$	Reject H_0
Sample1 from Aug 1 - Aug 14 Sample2 from Aug 15 - Aug 31	543.38	712.34	1.960	Yes
Sample1 from Aug 15 - Aug 31 Sample2 from Sept 1 - Sept 14	2534.01	3326.76	1.960	Yes
Sample1 from Sept 1 - Sept 14 Sample2 from Sept 15 - Sept 30	711.71	933.42	1.960	Yes
Sample1 from Sept 15 - Sept 30 Sample2 from Oct 1 - Oct 14	3046.27	3999.55	1.960	Yes
Sample1 from Oct 1 - Oct 14 Sample2 from Oct 15 - Oct 31	8386.10	11012.68	1.960	Yes
Sample1 from Oct 15 - Oct 31 Sample2 from Nov 1 - Nov 14	30567.86	40145.39	1.960	Yes
Sample1 from Nov 1 - Nov 14 Sample2 from Nov 15 - Nov 30	21585.54	28348.34	1.960	Yes
Sample1 from Nov 15 - Nov 30 Sample2 from Dec 1 - Dec 14	21001.86	27581.75	1.960	Yes
Sample1 from Dec 1 - Dec 14 Sample2 Dec 15 - Dec 31	7451.29	9784.94	1.960	Yes

Table 5.6: Results for K-sample AD test with $K = 2$ for a sequence of biweekly periods. The results pertain to the second dimension of each sample. T^{norm} comes from Table 5.1 with α=0.05 and μ_N = 1.

5.2 User Density Distribution

Figures from 5.1 to 5.10 depict estimated user density PDFs, $\hat{p}(\boldsymbol{x})$, for each biweekly period. The figures' $\hat{p}(\boldsymbol{x})$ axes corresponds to the estimated probability for a given latitude and longitude. Also, the $\hat{p}(\boldsymbol{x})$ axes have upper limits of $4 * 10^{-7}$ to help visualize both high-density and low-density peaks of the user density distribution. Appendix A.2 shows plots with an upper limit of $4 * 10^{-6}$ for $\hat{p}(\boldsymbol{x})$ axes. The grey regions in the plots represent $\hat{p}(\boldsymbol{x})$ values below $1.0 * 10^{-8}$. Each pair of subsequent biweekly user density $\hat{p}(\boldsymbol{x})$ estimates shown in the Figures 5.1 to 5.10 were visually compared and the results were validated with the AD test (Tables 5.2 to 5.6). The user density estimate for August 1-14 and August 15-31 (Figures 5.1 and 5.2) shows variability in the number, shape, and location of the peaks. It is concluded from the AD test results (Tables 5.5 and 5.6) that the changes in user densities are statistically significant and the user densities are considered non-stationary. Similarly, August 15-31 and September 1-14 (Figure 5.3), September 1-14 and September 15-30 (Figure 5.4), September 15-30 and October 1-14 (Figure 5.5) also show significant variation in user densities. Therefore, it is concluded from the AD test results (Tables 5.5 and 5.6) that the changes in user densities are statistically significant and the user densities are considered non-stationary.

Due to high volume, data from October 15th onward is analyzed in shards, with varying numbers of shards being required for each biweekly period. The data for these sharded periods was analyzed to first determine statistical similarity between the shards within the same period and then to determine similarities across periods. For the period of October 15-31, the data shards in Figures 5.6a and 5.6b show strong similarities in the number, shape, and location of peaks. The AD test results shown in Tables 5.2 and 5.3 confirm that the user densities of the shards in period October 15-31 are statistically similar and have the same distribution. A similar conclusion is drawn for shards in periods November 15-30 (Figure 5.8), December 1-14 (Figure 5.9), and December 15-31 (Figure 5.10). For the period of November 1-14, the data shard in Figure 5.7c shows more variability with respect to the number of peaks as compared to shards in Figures 5.7a and 5.7b. The AD test results from Table 5.4 confirm that Shard no. 3 is statisitically different from Shard no. 1 and 2.

User density estimates for a pair of subsequent biweekly periods from October 15th onward were visually compared using the periods' representative sample (i.e., Shard no. 1, see Subsection 5.1.3). For October 15-31 (Figure 5.6a) and November 1-14 (Figure 5.7a), November 1-14 and November 15-30 (Figure 5.8a), November15-30 and December 1-14 (Figure 5.9a), December 1-14 and December 15-31 (Figure 5.10a), the user densities showed a significant variation. Also, the AD test results (Tables 5.5 and 5.6) confirm that the user densities are statistically different and non-stationary.

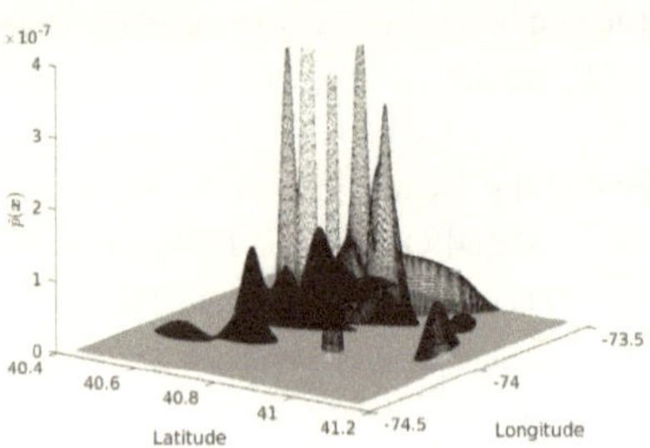

Figure 5.1: $\hat{p}(\boldsymbol{x})$ user density estimate for August 1-August 14, 2018.

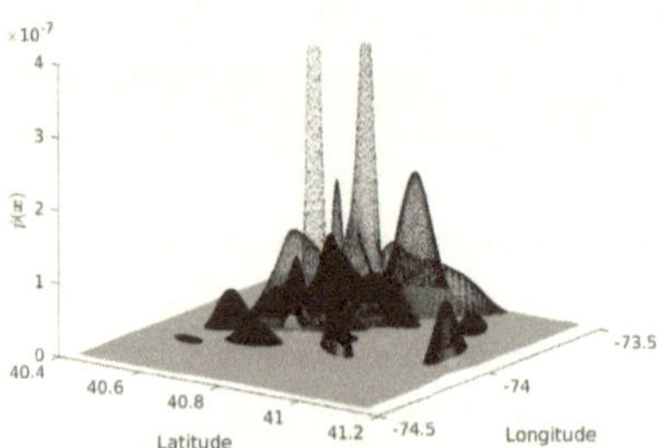

Figure 5.2: $\hat{p}(\boldsymbol{x})$ user density estimate for August 15-August 31, 2018.

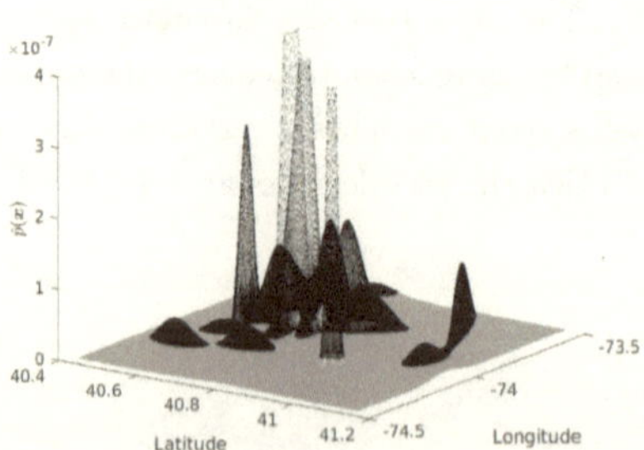

Figure 5.3: $\hat{p}(\boldsymbol{x})$ user density estimate for September 1-September 14, 2018.

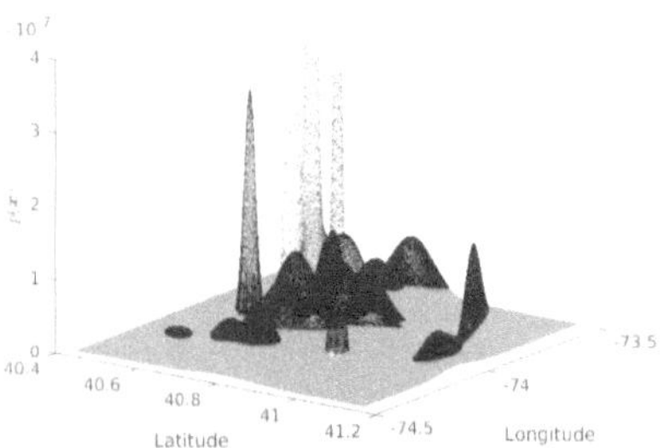

Figure 5.4: $\hat{p}(\boldsymbol{x})$ user density estimate for September 15-September 30, 2018.

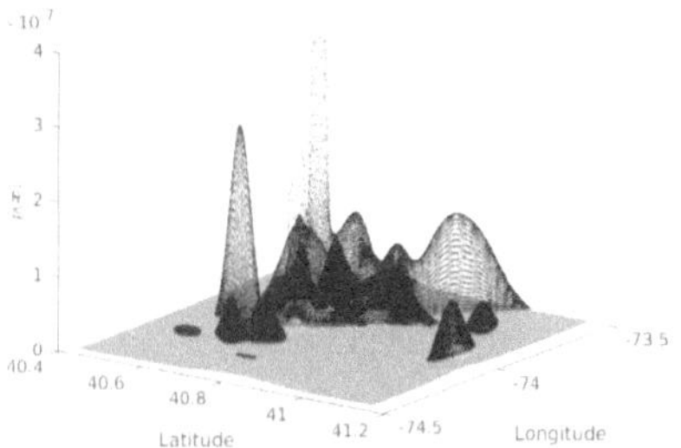

Figure 5.5: $\hat{p}(\boldsymbol{x})$ user density estimate for October 1-October 14, 2018.

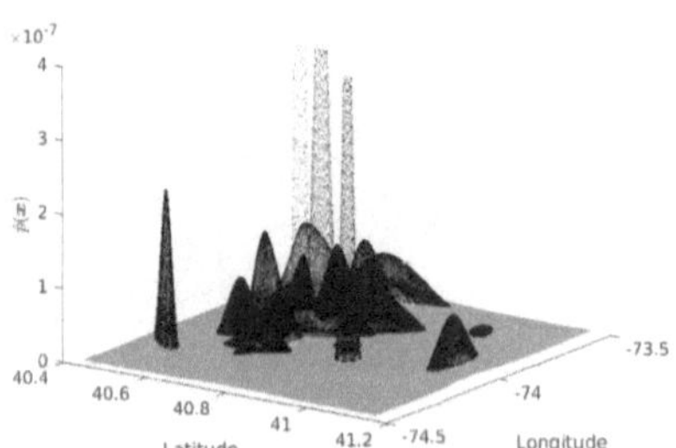

(a) $\hat{p}(\boldsymbol{x})$ user density estimate for October 15-October 31 for data Shard no. 1.

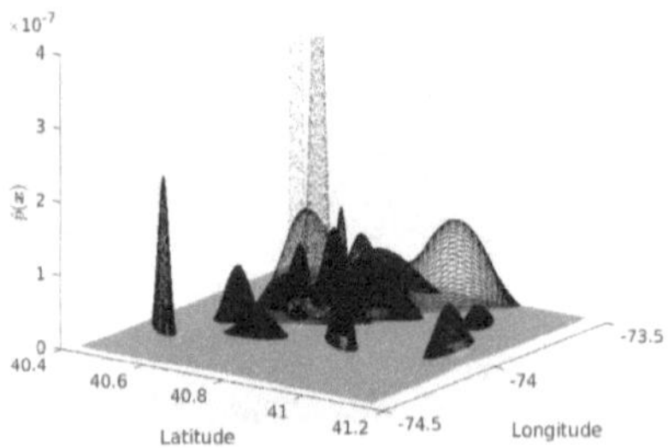

(b) $\hat{p}(\boldsymbol{x})$ user density estimate for October 15-October 31 for data Shard no. 2.

Figure 5.6: $\hat{p}(\boldsymbol{x})$ user density estimate for October 15-October 31, 2018.

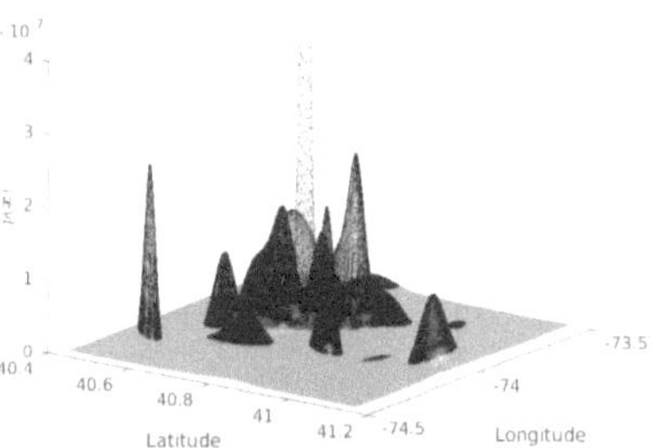

(a) $\hat{p}(\boldsymbol{x})$ user density estimate for November 1-November 14 for data Shard no. 1.

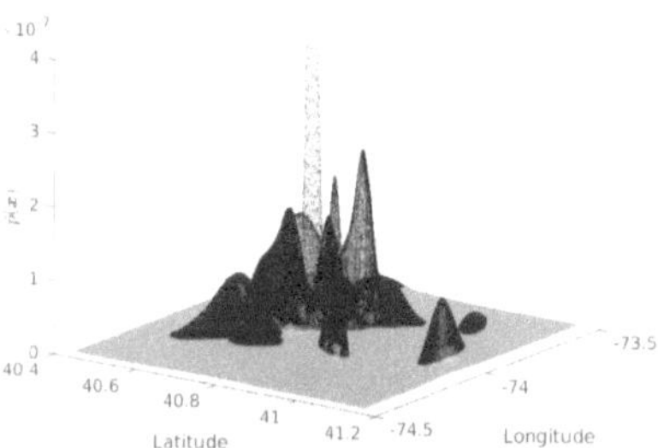

(b) $\hat{p}(\boldsymbol{x})$ user density estimate for November 1-November 14 for data Shard no. 2.

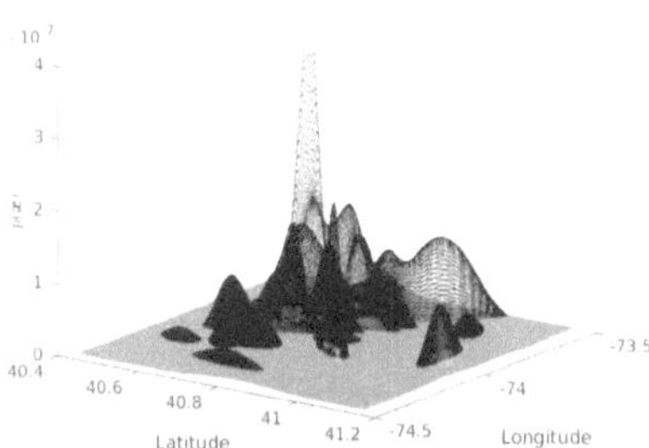

(c) $\hat{p}(\boldsymbol{x})$ user density estimate for November 1-November 14 for data Shard no. 3.

Figure 5.7: $\hat{p}(\boldsymbol{x})$ user density estimate for November 1-November 14, 2018.

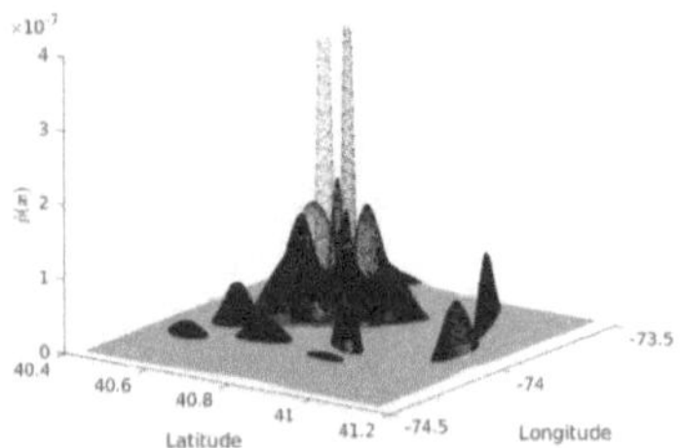

(a) $\hat{p}(\boldsymbol{x})$ user density estimate for November 15-November 30 for data Shard no. 1.

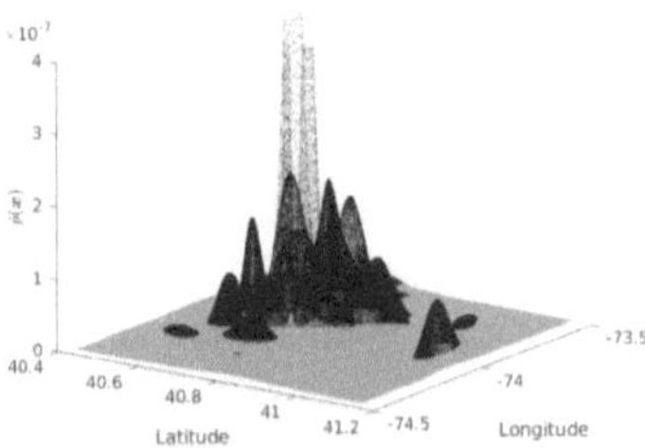

(b) $\hat{p}(\boldsymbol{x})$ user density estimate for November 15-November 30 for data Shard no. 2.

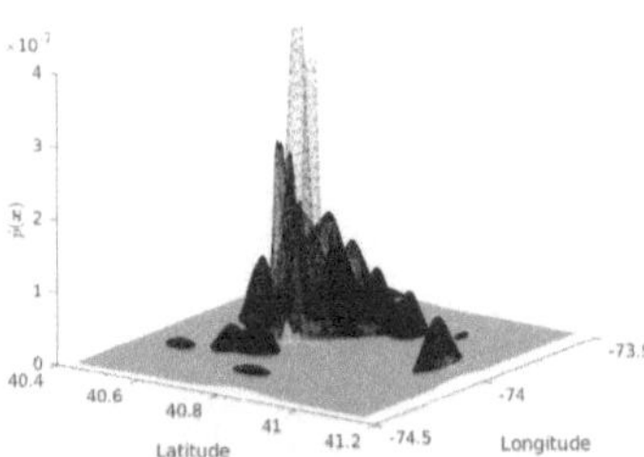

(c) $\hat{p}(\boldsymbol{x})$ user density estimate for November 15-November 30 for data Shard no. 3.

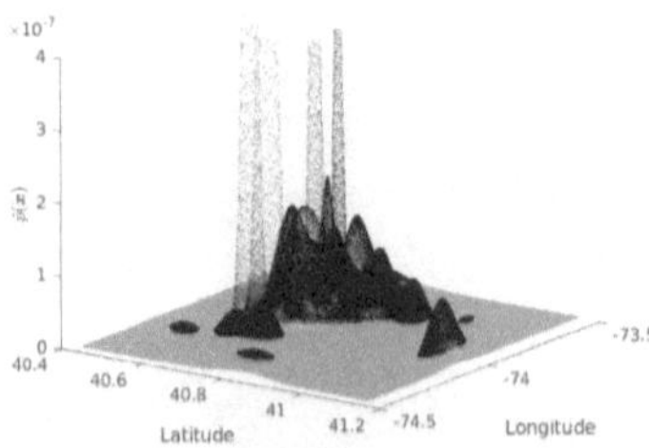

(d) $\hat{p}(\boldsymbol{x})$ user density estimate for November 15-November 30 for data Shard no. 4.

Figure 5.8: $\hat{p}(\boldsymbol{x})$ user density estimate for November 15-November 30, 2018.

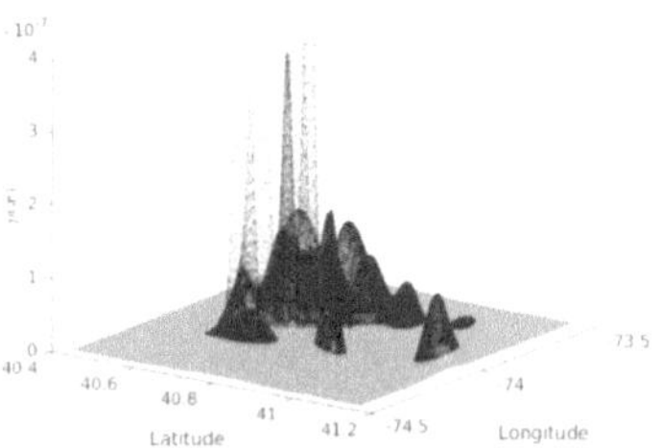

(a) $\hat{p}(\boldsymbol{x})$ user density estimate for December 1-December 14 for data Shard no. 1.

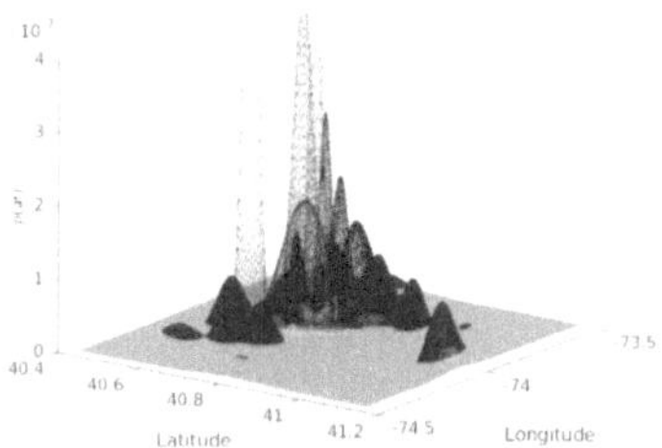

(b) $\hat{p}(\boldsymbol{x})$ user density estimate for December 1-December 14 for data Shard no. 2.

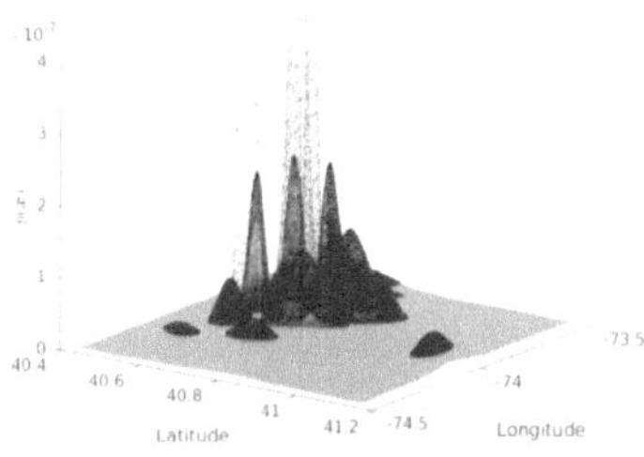

(c) $\hat{p}(\boldsymbol{x})$ user density estimate for December 1-December 14 for data Shard no. 3.

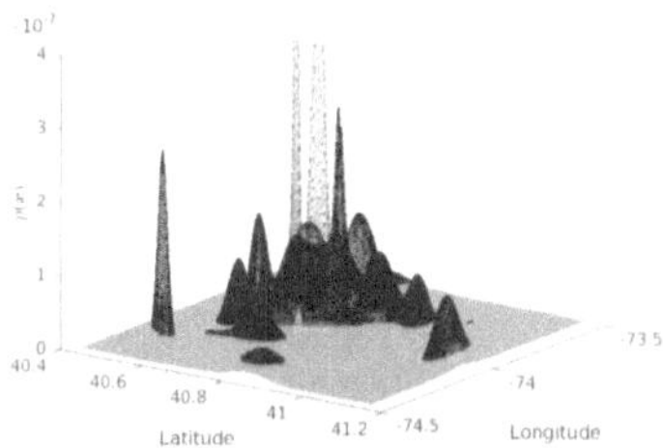

(d) $\hat{p}(\boldsymbol{x})$ user density estimate for December 1-December 14 for data Shard no. 4.

Figure 5.9: $\hat{p}(\boldsymbol{x})$ user density estimate for December 1-December 14, 2018.

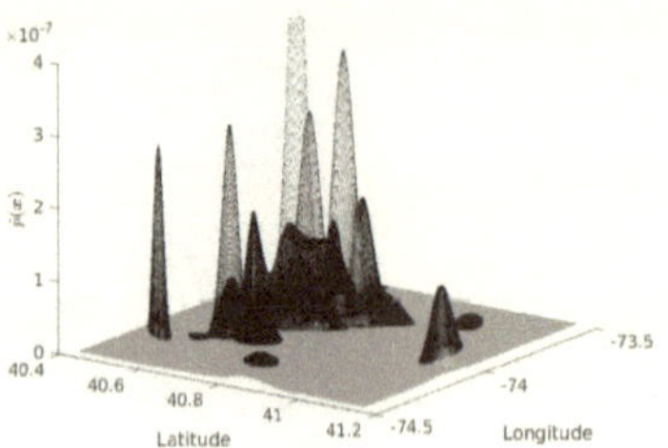

(a) $\hat{p}(\boldsymbol{x})$ user density estimate for December 15-December 31 for data Shard no. 1.

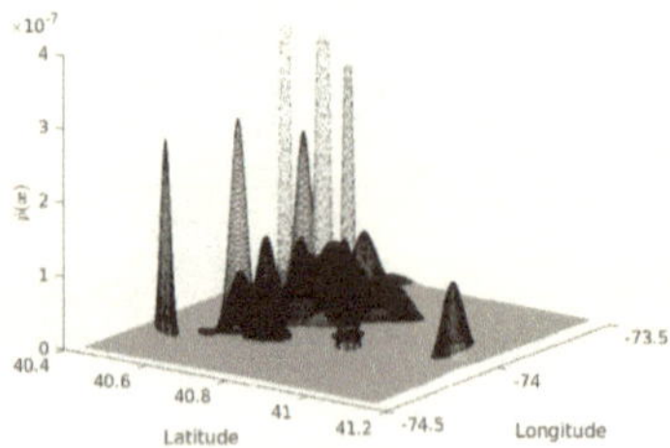

(b) $\hat{p}(\boldsymbol{x})$ user density estimate for December 15-December 31 for data Shard no. 2.

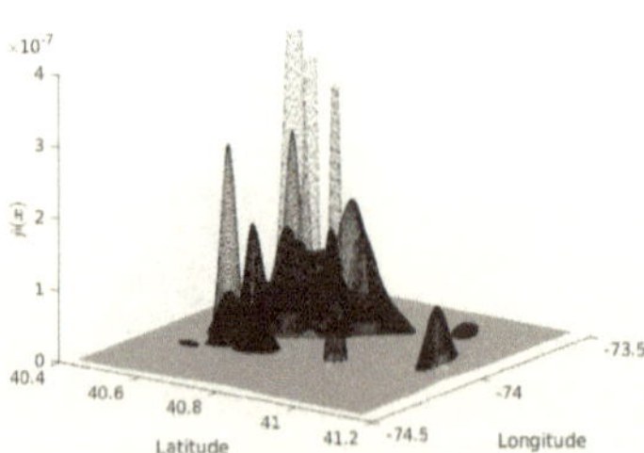

(c) $\hat{p}(\boldsymbol{x})$ user density estimate for December 15-December 31 for data Shard no. 3.

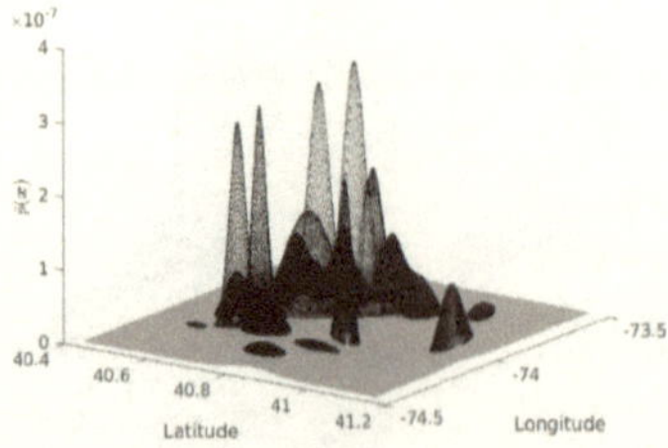

(d) $\hat{p}(\boldsymbol{x})$ user density estimate for December 15-December 31 for data Shard no. 4.

Figure 5.10: $\hat{p}(\boldsymbol{x})$ user density estimate for December 15-December 31, 2018.

5.3 Quality of Service Analysis of Mobile Users

Due to high volume, the data used for Quality of Service analysis was selected from every other biweekly period. Furthermore, data within each selected biweekly period was downsampled by a factor of 3, i.e., every third sample observation was chosen for the analysis. Quality of Service analysis was then conducted by partitioning the data into three distinct user densities: high, medium, and low. Table 5.7 shows the threshold values for data partitioning based on the top 33% and bottom 33% of user density estimates, $\hat{p}(x)$. Data with $\hat{p}(x)$ above the top 33% threshold corresponds to high density, $\hat{p}(x)$ between the top and bottom 33% threshold corresponds to medium density, and $\hat{p}(x)$ below the bottom 33% threshold corresponds to low density. Figures 5.11 to 5.15 show different user densities for the selected biweekly periods. The figures' $\hat{p}(x)$ axes corresponds to the estimated probability for a given latitude and longitude. The blue, green, and red regions correspond to areas of high, medium, and low user densities. From August 1-14 (Figure 5.11) to September 1-14 (Figure 5.12), the geographical locations of high and medium density regions change but low density region remains consistent. Similar observations are made from September 1-14 to October 1-14 (Figure 5.13), October 1-14 to November 1-14 (Figure 5.14), and November 1-14 to December 1-14 (Figure 5.15). Furthermore, the user density peaks vary from one biweekly period to the next. For example, the high density peaks for October 1-14 are relatively higher, i.e., by an order of magnitude, than for September 1-14 (see Table 5.7, top 33% $\hat{p}(x)$ threshold). Similar observations are made between August 1-14 to September 1-14, October 1-14 to November 1-14, and November 1-14 to December 1-14 (see Table 5.7, top 33% $\hat{p}(x)$ threshold).

Data from selected biweekly periods	Top 33% $\hat{p}(x)$ threshold	Bottom 33% $\hat{p}(x)$ threshold
Aug 1 - Aug 14	$6.2 * 10^{-07}$	$3.0 * 10^{-07}$
Sept 1 - Sept 14	$4.2 * 10^{-07}$	$2.1 * 10^{-07}$
Oct 1 - Oct 14	$1.9 * 10^{-06}$	$9.2 * 10^{-07}$
Nov 1 - Nov 14	$5.0 * 10^{-07}$	$2.4 * 10^{-07}$
Dec 1 - Dec 14	$8.8 * 10^{-07}$	$4.3 * 10^{-07}$

Table 5.7: Top and bottom threshold values for $\hat{p}(x)$. The threshold values partition the data into high density (data with $\hat{p}(x)$ values more than top 33% threshold), medium density (data with $\hat{p}(x)$ values between top and bottom 33% threshold) and low density (data with $\hat{p}(x)$ less than bottom 33% threshold).

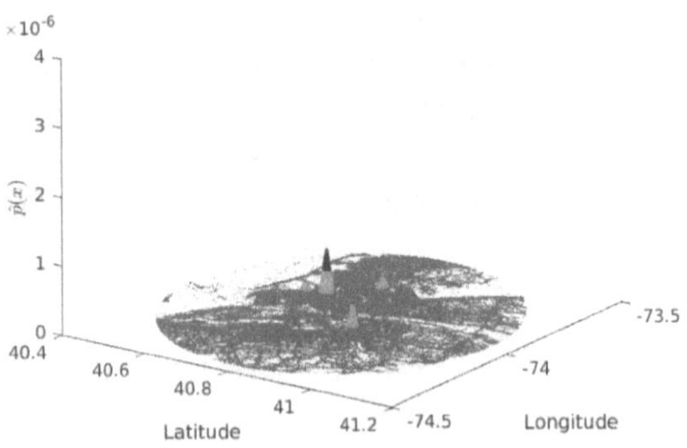

Figure 5.11: Mobile users representing high density (blue), medium density (green), and low density (red) regions for the period of August 1-August 14, 2018.

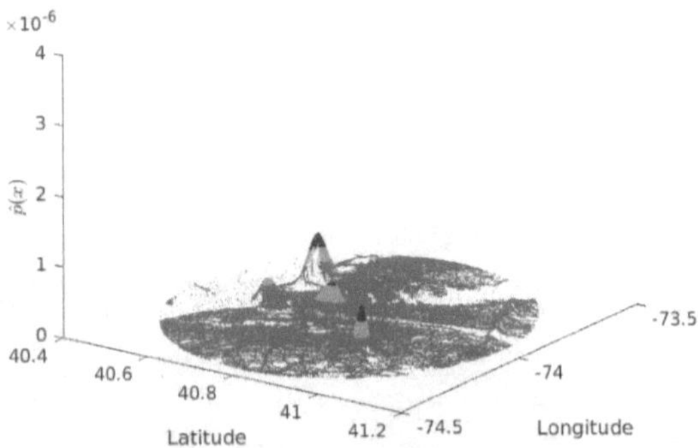

Figure 5.12: Mobile users representing high density (blue), medium density (green), and low density (red) regions for the period of September 1-September 14, 2018.

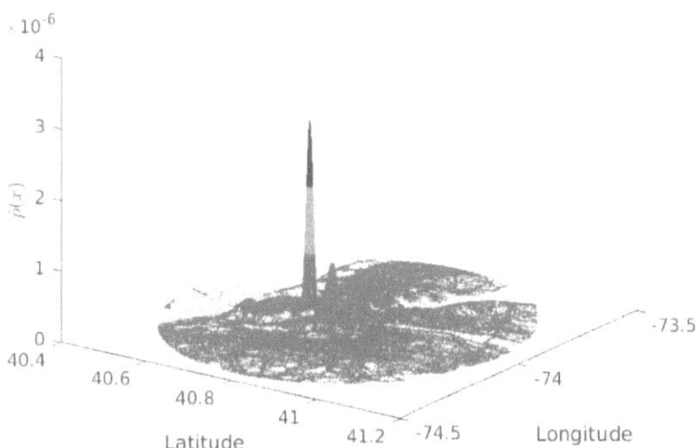

Figure 5.13: Mobile users representing high density (blue), medium density (green), and low density (red) regions for the period of October 1-October 14, 2018.

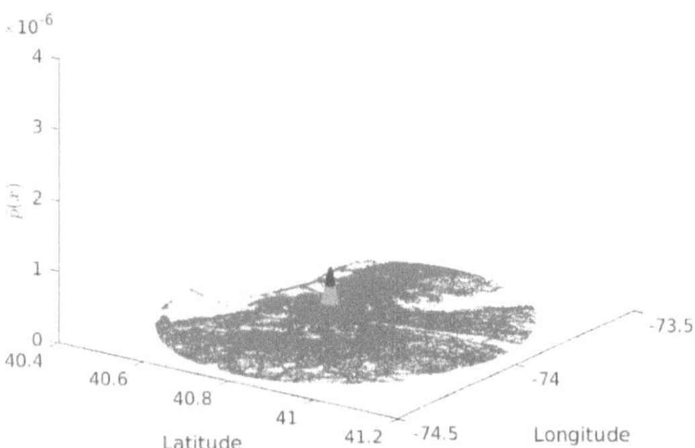

Figure 5.14: Mobile users representing high density (blue), medium density (green), and low density (red) regions for the period of November 1-November 14, 2018.

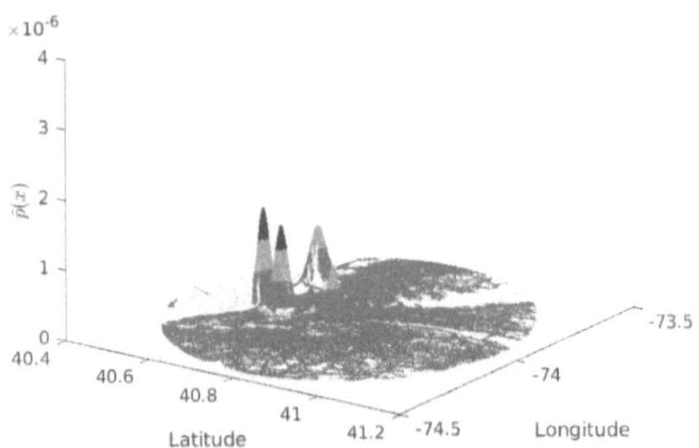

Figure 5.15: Mobile users representing high density (blue), medium density (green), and low density (red) regions for the period of December 1-December 14, 2018.

5.3.1   Comparison of QoS Parameters

Quality of Service parameters analyzed are download throughput, upload throughput, average latency, average jitter, and signal strength. Each QoS parameter was analyzed with respect to data partitioned into high, medium, and low user densities.

5.3.1.1   Download Throughput

Figure 5.16 shows histograms representing download throughput of users in high, medium, and low density regions. The histograms have a bin size of 5 Mbps. As the user count is variable for each density region within each biweekly period, the histograms have a normalized bin count. The number of users in each bin was normalized by the total number of users present in each density region for each biweekly period. Download throughput of users was analyzed by dividing the users into four different QoS levels such as excellent (40+ Mbps), good (25-40 Mbps), adequate (10-25 Mbps), and poor (0-10 Mbps). Tables 5.8, 5.9, and 5.10 show percentage of users receiving different levels of download throughput in high, medium, and low density regions.

5.3.1.1.1 High Density For the biweekly periods between August 1, 2018, and December 1-14, the histograms for the high density region show high variability with respect to the number of users getting download throughput (Figure 5.16) as compared to medium and low density regions. These observations are confirmed with Table 5.8, where the standard deviation of each QoS level is higher for the high density region as compared to medium and low density regions (Tables 5.9 and 5.10). The histograms for the high density region are right-skewed and decay quickly as there are less users receiving higher download throughputs. Table 5.8 shows that for August 1-14, October 1-14, and November 1-14, more users receive high QoS levels (i.e., 40+ Mbps) as compared to other biweekly periods. Also, the histograms for these biweekly periods decay slowly as compared to other periods. Furthermore, there is a significant increase in the number of users receiving adequate QoS levels (i.e., 10 to 25 Mbps) for October 1-14 and December 1-14 as compared to other biweekly periods. Note, as the users' QoS levels improve for October 1-14, the user density increases and is the highest for this period than any other biweekly period (Figures 5.11 to 5.15 and Table 5.7). Also, for September 1-14 and December 1-14, fewer users receive download throughput of 40+ Mbps (Table 5.8); it is observed that the density peaks for these periods have a wider spread as compared to other biweekly periods (Figures 5.11 to 5.15).

5.3.1.1.2 Medium Density The histograms for the medium density region decay slowly as compared to the high density region suggesting there are more users receiving higher download throughputs (Figure 5.16). For September 1-14 and October 1-14, more users receive high QoS levels (i.e., 25 to 40+ Mbps) as compared to other biweekly periods (Table 5.9). Furthermore, there is a decrease in number of users receiving high QoS levels for November 1-14 (25 to 40+ Mbps) and December 1-14 (10 to 25 Mbps and 40+ Mbps). As mentioned earlier, both September 1-14 and December 1-14 have density peaks with a wider spread (Figures 5.12 and 5.15) but for December 1-14, users in both high and medium density regions experience low QoS levels whereas for September 1-14, only high density users experience low levels of QoS.

5.3.1.1.3 Low Density The histograms for low density region (Figure 5.16) are right-skewed and decay less quickly as compared to high and medium density regions suggesting more users receive higher download throughputs. Also, they show less variability as compared to high and medium density regions. Similar to medium density region, September 1-14 and October 1-14 periods have more users receiving high QoS levels (i.e., 25 to 40+ Mbps) as compared to other biweekly periods (Table 5.10). Also, there is a decrease in number of users receiving high QoS levels for November 1-14 (25 to 40+ Mbps) and December 1-14 (40+ Mbps) as compared to other biweekly periods (Table 5.10). Furthermore, there more users experiencing download throughput of 40+ Mbps for the low density region (Table 5.10) than medium and high density regions (Tables 5.8 and 5.9).

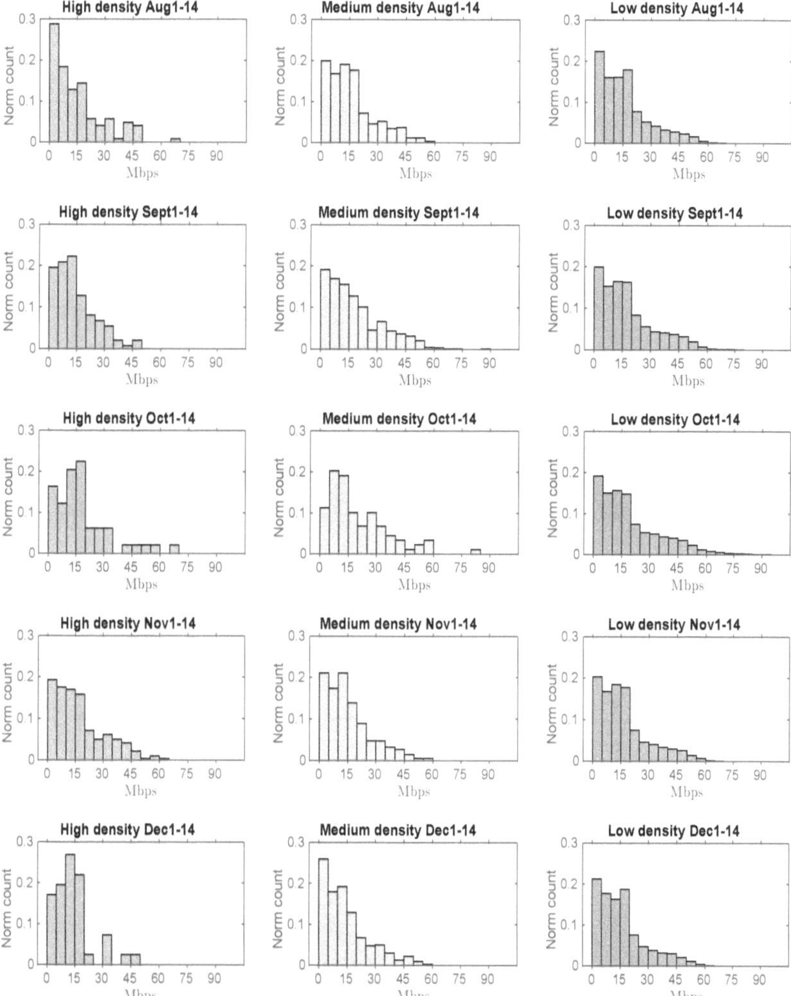

Figure 5.16: Histograms representing download throughput of mobile users in high, medium, and low density regions for biweekly periods between August 1, 2018, and December 14, 2018.

Biweekly period	0 to 10 Mbps	10 to 25 Mbps	25 to 40 Mbps	40+ Mbps
Aug 1 - Aug 14	47.20%	32.80%	10.40%	9.60%
Sept 1 - Sept 14	40.27%	42.95%	14.09%	2.68%
Oct 1 - Oct 14	28.57%	48.98%	12.24%	10.20%
Nov 1 - Nov 14	36.73%	39.65%	16.04%	7.58%
Dec 1 - Dec 14	36.59%	51.22%	7.32%	4.88%
Average	37.87%	43.12%	12.02%	6.99%
Median	36.73%	42.95%	12.24%	7.58%
Standard deviation	6.75%	7.39%	3.36%	3.18%

Table 5.8: Percentage of mobile users experiencing download throughput in high density regions for biweekly periods from August 1, 2018, to December 14, 2018. The users are divided into poor (0 to 10 Mbps), adequate (10 to 25 Mbps), good (25 to 40 Mbps), and excellent (40+ Mbps) QoS levels.

Biweekly period	0 to 10 Mbps	10 to 25 Mbps	25 to 40 Mbps	40+ Mbps
Aug 1 - Aug 14	36.75%	43.87%	13.11%	6.27%
Sept 1 - Sept 14	36.04%	38.35%	15.53%	10.08%
Oct 1 - Oct 14	31.46%	35.96%	21.35%	11.24%
Nov 1 - Nov 14	38.37%	43.81%	12.62%	5.20%
Dec 1 - Dec 14	43.78%	38.81%	12.69%	4.73%
Average	37.28%	40.16%	15.06%	7.50%
Median	36.75%	38.81%	13.11%	6.27%
Standard deviation	4.45%	3.53%	3.71%	2.96%

Table 5.9: Percentage of mobile users experiencing download throughput in medium density regions for biweekly periods from August 1, 2018, to December 14, 2018. The users are divided into poor (0 to 10 Mbps), adequate (10 to 25 Mbps), good (25 to 40 Mbps), and excellent (40+ Mbps) QoS levels.

Biweekly period	0 to 10 Mbps	10 to 25 Mbps	25 to 40 Mbps	40+ Mbps
Aug 1 - Aug 14	38.42%	41.70%	12.53%	7.34%
Sept 1 - Sept 14	35.10%	40.96%	13.96%	9.98%
Oct 1 - Oct 14	34.23%	37.91%	14.67%	13.19%
Nov 1 - Nov 14	36.87%	43.49%	11.88%	7.76%
Dec 1 - Dec 14	38.89%	42.58%	11.67%	6.87%
Average	36.70%	41.33%	12.94%	9.03%
Median	36.87%	41.70%	12.53%	7.76%
Standard deviation	2.03%	2.13%	1.32%	2.62%

Table 5.10: Percentage of mobile users experiencing download throughput in low density regions for biweekly periods from August 1, 2018, to December 14, 2018. The users are divided into poor (0 to 10 Mbps), adequate (10 to 25 Mbps), good (25 to 40 Mbps), and excellent (40+ Mbps) QoS levels.

5.3.1.2 Upload Throughput

Figure 5.17 shows histograms representing upload throughput of users in high, medium, and low density regions. The histograms have a bin size of 5 Mbps. As the user count is variable for each density region within each biweekly period, the histograms have a normalized bin count. The number of users in each bin was normalized by the total number of users present in each density region for each biweekly period. Upload throughput of users was analyzed by dividing the users into four different QoS levels such as excellent (25+ Mbps), good (15-25 Mbps), adequate (10-15 Mbps), and poor (0-10 Mbps). Tables 5.11, 5.12, and 5.13 show percentage of users receiving different levels of upload throughput in high, medium, and low density regions.

5.3.1.2.1 High Density The average number of users getting different levels of upload throughputs in the high density region (Table 5.11) is more variable as compared to medium and low density regions (Tables 5.12 and 5.13). Also, for September 1-14, October 1-14, and November 1-14, the number of users receiving higher QoS levels increases (15 to 25+ Mbps) as compared to other periods. Furthermore, for December 1-14, there is an increase in the number of users receiving upload throughput of 10 to 15 Mbps. The histograms for the high density region are right skewed and most of the users receive upload throughput of 0-15 Mbps (Figure 5.17) for each biweekly period.

5.3.1.2.2 Medium Density As compared to high density region, histograms for the medium density region decay less quickly as more users get higher upload throughputs (Figure 5.17). For October 1-14, more users receive higher QoS levels (10 to 25 Mbps) as compared to other biweekly periods (Table 5.12). Also, more users experience higher upload throughputs (15 to 25+ Mbps) in the medium density region (Table 5.12) as compared to high and low density regions (Tables 5.11 and 5.13).

5.3.1.2.3 Low Density The histograms for the low density region are less variable as compared to high and medium density regions (Figure 5.17). Furthermore, the number of users receiving different upload throughput levels is consistent for each biweekly period (Table 5.13).

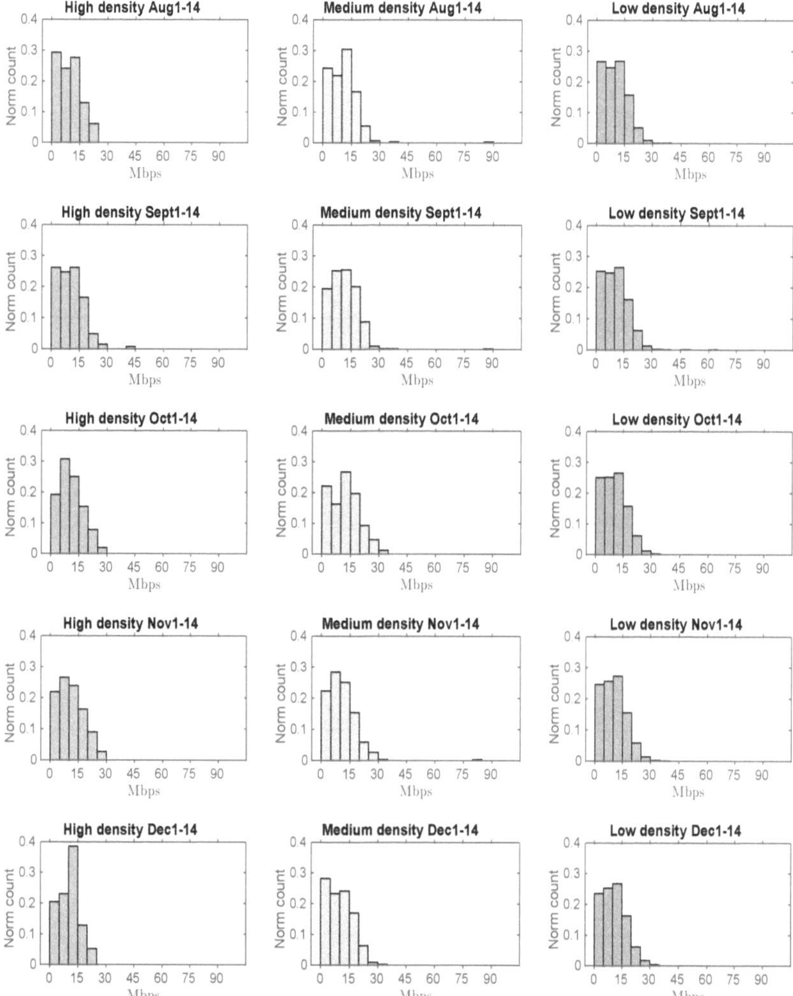

Figure 5.17: Histograms representing upload throughput of mobile users in high, medium, and low density regions for biweekly periods between August 1, 2018, and December 14, 2018.

Biweekly period	0 to 10 Mbps	10 to 15 Mbps	15 to 25 Mbps	25+ Mbps
Aug 1 - Aug 14	53.45%	27.59%	18.97%	0.00%
Sept 1 - Sept 14	50.68%	26.03%	21.23%	2.05%
Oct 1 - Oct 14	50.00%	25.00%	23.08%	1.92%
Nov 1 - Nov 14	48.34%	23.84%	25.17%	2.65%
Dec 1 - Dec 14	43.59%	38.46%	17.95%	0.00%
Average	49.21%	28.18%	21.28%	1.33%
Median	50.00%	26.03%	21.23%	1.92%
Standard deviation	3.64%	5.91%	2.95%	1.24%

Table 5.11: Percentage of mobile users experiencing upload throughput in high density regions for biweekly periods from August 1, 2018, to December 14, 2018. The users are divided into poor (0 to 10 Mbps), adequate (10 to 15 Mbps), good (15 to 25 Mbps), and excellent (25+ Mbps) QoS levels.

Biweekly period	0 to 10 Mbps	10 to 15 Mbps	15 to 25 Mbps	25+ Mbps
Aug 1 - Aug 14	46.20%	30.40%	22.19%	1.22%
Sept 1 - Sept 14	44.49%	25.49%	28.80%	1.23%
Oct 1 - Oct 14	38.37%	26.74%	29.07%	5.81%
Nov 1 - Nov 14	50.64%	25.06%	21.23%	3.07%
Dec 1 - Dec 14	51.49%	24.12%	23.31%	1.08%
Average	46.24%	26.36%	24.92%	2.48%
Median	46.20%	25.49%	23.31%	1.23%
Standard deviation	5.29%	2.44%	3.74%	2.04%

Table 5.12: Percentage of mobile users experiencing upload throughput in medium density regions for biweekly periods from August 1, 2018, to December 14, 2018. The users are divided into poor (0 to 10 Mbps), adequate (10 to 15 Mbps), good (15 to 25 Mbps), and excellent (25+ Mbps) QoS levels.

Biweekly period	0 to 10 Mbps	10 to 15 Mbps	15 to 25 Mbps	25+ Mbps
Aug 1 - Aug 14	51.25%	26.73%	20.80%	1.22%
Sept 1 - Sept 14	49.84%	26.34%	22.26%	1.57%
Oct 1 - Oct 14	50.16%	26.47%	21.79%	1.57%
Nov 1 - Nov 14	50.01%	27.16%	21.22%	1.60%
Dec 1 - Dec 14	48.79%	26.76%	22.36%	2.10%
Average	50.01%	26.69%	21.69%	1.61%
Median	50.01%	26.73%	21.79%	1.57%
Standard deviation	0.88%	0.32%	0.67%	0.31%

Table 5.13: Percentage of mobile users experiencing upload throughput in low density regions for biweekly periods from August 1, 2018, to December 14, 2018. The users are divided into poor (0 to 10 Mbps), adequate (10 to 15 Mbps), good (15 to 25 Mbps), and excellent (25+ Mbps) QoS levels.

5.3.1.3 Latency Average

Figure 5.18 shows histograms representing average latency of users in high, medium, and low density regions. The histograms have a bin size of 5 millisecs. As the user count is variable for each density region within each biweekly period, the histograms have a normalized bin count. The number of users in each bin was normalized by the total number of users present in each density region for each biweekly period. Average latency of users was analyzed by dividing the users into four different QoS levels such as excellent (10 to 25 ms), good (25 to 50 ms), adequate (50 to 75 ms), and poor (75+ ms). Tables 5.14, 5.15, and 5.16 show percentage of users receiving different levels of average latency in high, medium, and low density regions.

5.3.1.3.1 High Density For the biweekly periods of October 1-14, November 1-14, and December 1-14, the number of users experiencing excellent latency (10 to 25 ms) is higher as compared to other biweekly periods (Table 5.14). From August 1-14 to December 1-14, the number of users experiencing adequate to poor latency (50 to 75+ ms) decreases (Table 5.14). This suggests that with each passing biweekly period, the users experience better latencies. The histograms for the high density region are right-skewed and most of the users have a latency of 10 to 50 millisecs, except for December 1-14, where most users experience latencies between 10 to 25 millisecs (Figure 5.18).

5.3.1.3.2 Medium Density As compared to high and low density regions (Tables 5.14 and 5.16), more users in the medium density region experience better latencies (10 to 25 ms) (Table 5.15). Similar to high density region, the number of users experiencing excellent latency increases drastically for the period of December 1-14 as compared to other periods (Table 5.15). The histograms for the medium density region are right-skewed with most of the users experiencing latencies from 10 to 50 millisecs except for December 1-14, where most of the users experience latencies between 10 to 25 millisecs (Figure 5.18).

5.3.1.3.3 Low Density For the low density region (Table 5.16), there are fewer users experiencing better latencies (10 to 25 ms) as compared to high and medium density regions (Tables 5.14 and 5.15). Also, the number of users experiencing excellent latency (10 to 25 ms) increases for the period of December 1-14 in the low density region similar to high and medium density regions. Furthermore, from August 1-14 to December 1-14, the number of users experiencing adequate to poor latency (50 to 75+ ms) decreases (Table 5.16). The histograms for the low density region are right-skewed with most of the users experiencing latencies from 10 to 50 millisecs except for December 1-14, where most of the users experience latencies between 10 to 25 millisecs (Figure 5.18).

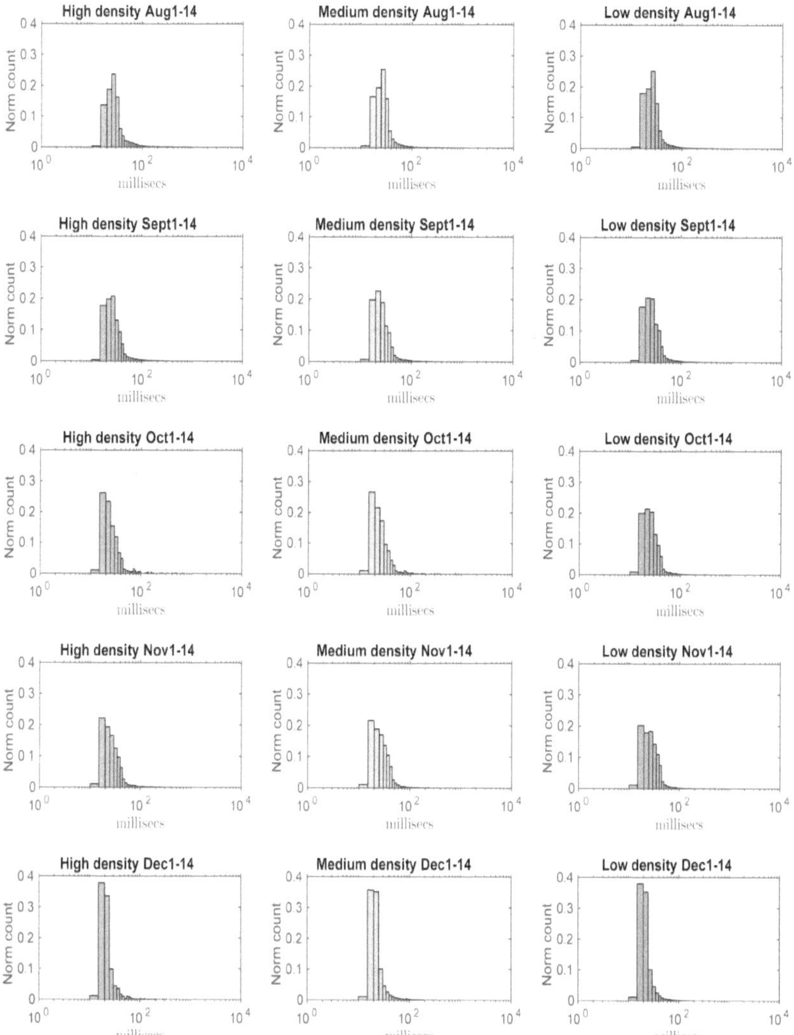

Figure 5.18: Histograms representing average latency of mobile users in high, medium, and low density regions for biweekly periods between August 1, 2018, and December 14, 2018.

Biweekly period	10 to 25 millisecs	25 to 50 millisecs	50 to 75 millisecs	75+ millisecs
Aug 1 - Aug 14	32.73%	51.32%	6.65%	9.31%
Sept 1 - Sept 14	37.87%	50.44%	4.82%	6.87%
Oct 1 - Oct 14	50.53%	39.86%	3.91%	5.69%
Nov 1 - Nov 14	42.47%	47.62%	3.84%	6.07%
Dec 1 - Dec 14	72.61%	20.34%	2.91%	4.14%
Average	47.24%	41.91%	4.43%	6.42%
Median	42.47%	47.62%	3.91%	6.07%
Standard deviation	15.62%	12.88%	1.41%	1.90%

Table 5.14: Percentage of mobile users experiencing average latency in high density regions for biweekly periods from August 1, 2018, to December 14, 2018. The users are divided into excellent (10 to 25 ms), good (25 to 50 ms), adequate (50 to 75 ms), and poor (75+ ms) QoS levels.

Biweekly period	10 to 25 millisecs	25 to 50 millisecs	50 to 75 millisecs	75+ millisecs
Aug 1 - Aug 14	36.62%	51.16%	4.49%	7.73%
Sept 1 - Sept 14	42.93%	46.20%	3.96%	6.91%
Oct 1 - Oct 14	49.13%	41.54%	3.11%	6.22%
Nov 1 - Nov 14	41.32%	50.22%	3.86%	4.61%
Dec 1 - Dec 14	71.93%	19.87%	2.87%	5.32%
Average	48.39%	41.80%	3.66%	6.16%
Median	42.93%	46.20%	3.86%	6.22%
Standard deviation	13.90%	12.83%	0.66%	1.24%

Table 5.15: Percentage of mobile users experiencing average latency in medium density regions for biweekly periods from August 1, 2018, to December 14, 2018. The users are divided into excellent (10 to 25 ms), good (25 to 50 ms), adequate (50 to 75 ms), and poor (75+ ms) QoS levels.

Biweekly period	10 to 25 millisecs	25 to 50 millisecs	50 to 75 millisecs	75+ millisecs
Aug 1 - Aug 14	37.58%	50.18%	4.65%	7.58%
Sept 1 - Sept 14	38.75%	49.81%	4.32%	7.13%
Oct 1 - Oct 14	42.20%	50.45%	3.21%	4.14%
Nov 1 - Nov 14	39.18%	53.17%	3.51%	4.14%
Dec 1 - Dec 14	74.28%	19.69%	2.27%	3.75%
Average	46.40%	44.66%	3.59%	5.35%
Median	39.18%	50.18%	3.51%	4.14%
Standard deviation	15.68%	14.02%	0.94%	1.84%

Table 5.16: Percentage of mobile users experiencing average latency in low density regions for biweekly periods from August 1, 2018, to December 14, 2018. The users are divided into excellent (10 to 25 ms), good (25 to 50 ms), adequate (50 to 75 ms), and poor (75+ ms) QoS levels.

5.3.1.4 Jitter Average

Figure 5.19 shows histograms representing average jitter of users in high, medium, and low density regions. The histograms have a bin size of 1 millisec. As the user count is variable for each density region within each biweekly period, the histograms have a normalized bin count. The number of users in each bin was normalized by the total number of users present in each density region for each biweekly period. Average jitter of users was analyzed by dividing the users into four different QoS levels such as excellent (0 to 4 ms), good (4 to 10 ms), adequate (10 to 20 ms), and poor (20+ ms). Tables 5.17, 5.18, and 5.19 show percentage of users experiencing different levels of average jitter in high, medium, and low density regions.

5.3.1.4.1 High Density For the high density region, the number of users experiencing excellent jitter (0 to 4 ms) increases over each biweekly period (Table 5.17). However, nearly half of the users experience jitter between 4 to 10 ms for each biweekly period (Table 5.17). As compared to medium and low density regions (Tables 5.18 and 5.19), more users in the high density region experience poor jitter (20+ ms) (Table 5.17). The histograms for the high density region (Figure 5.19) are right-skewed and most of the users experience jitter from 0 to 10 ms.

5.3.1.4.2 Medium Density The histograms for the medium density region (Figure 5.19) look similar to the high density region, i.e., they are right-skewed and decay quickly with most of the users experiencing jitter between 0 and 10 ms. The average number of users experiencing different levels of jitter in the medium density region (Table 5.18) is also similar to high density region (Table 5.17). This suggests that the users in the high and medium density regions experience similar jitter.

5.3.1.4.3 Low density As compared to high and medium density regions (Tables 5.17 and 5.18), more users in the low density region experience better jitter (0 to 4 ms) (Table 5.19). Also, fewer users experience poor jitter (20+ ms) in the low density region (Table 5.19) as compared to medium and high density regions (Tables 5.17 and 5.18). The histograms for the low density region (Figure 5.19) are right-skewed and decay quickly suggesting that most users experience jitter from 0 to 10 ms. Also, the histograms are consistent throughout each biweekly period suggesting that different levels of jitter experienced by the users remain steady.

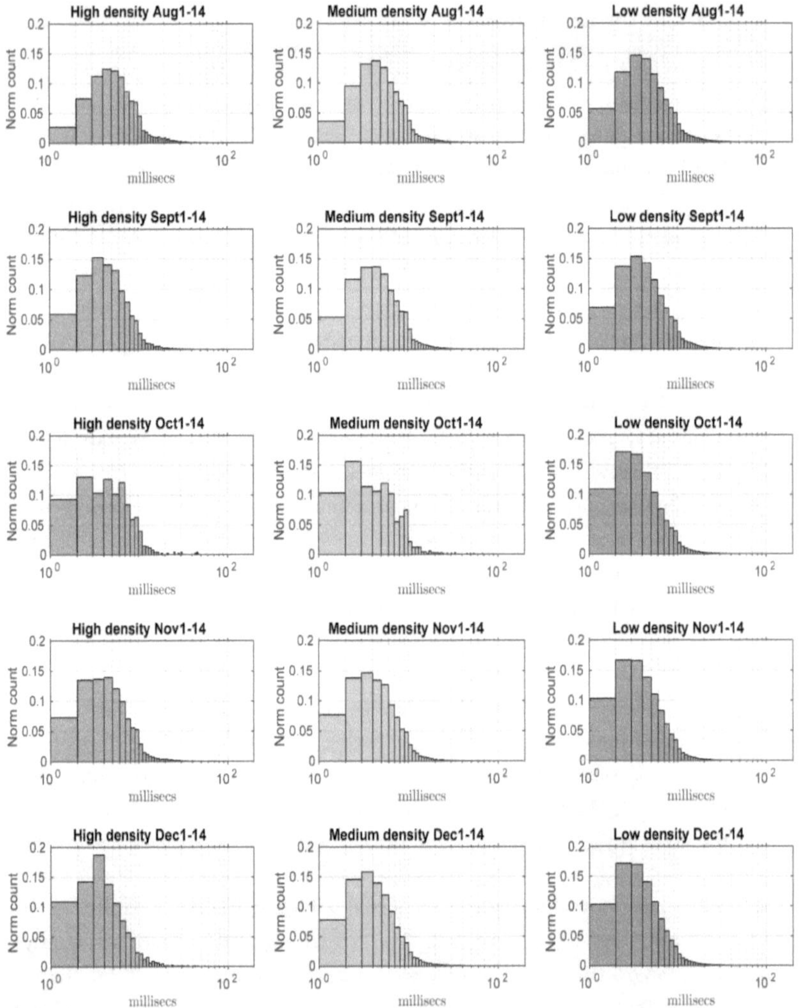

Figure 5.19: Histograms representing average jitter of mobile users in high, medium, and low density regions for biweekly periods between August 1, 2018, and December 14, 2018.

Biweekly period	0 to 4 millisecs	4 to 10 millisecs	10 to 20 millisecs	20+ millisecs
Aug 1 - Aug 14	21.50%	58.14%	15.07%	5.29%
Sept 1 - Sept 14	34.10%	54.93%	8.89%	2.09%
Oct 1 - Oct 14	33.39%	55.54%	9.29%	1.79%
Nov 1 - Nov 14	35.03%	53.57%	8.83%	2.58%
Dec 1 - Dec 14	46.00%	44.83%	7.89%	1.29%
Average	34.00%	53.40%	9.99%	2.60%
Median	34.10%	54.93%	8.89%	2.09%
Standard deviation	8.68%	5.07%	2.89%	1.57%

Table 5.17: Percentage of mobile users experiencing average jitter in high density regions for biweekly periods from August 1, 2018, to December 14, 2018. The users are divided into excellent (0 to 4 ms), good (4 to 10 ms), adequate (10 to 20 ms), and poor (20+ ms) QoS levels.

Biweekly period	0 to 4 millisecs	4 to 10 millisecs	10 to 20 millisecs	20+ millisecs
Aug 1 - Aug 14	26.76%	58.19%	12.12%	2.93%
Sept 1 - Sept 14	30.99%	56.08%	10.58%	2.35%
Oct 1 - Oct 14	38.61%	52.05%	7.35%	1.99%
Nov 1 - Nov 14	36.78%	52.56%	8.95%	1.70%
Dec 1 - Dec 14	39.14%	50.29%	8.48%	2.09%
Average	34.46%	53.84%	9.49%	2.21%
Median	36.78%	52.56%	8.95%	2.09%
Standard deviation	5.38%	3.21%	1.87%	0.46%

Table 5.18: Percentage of mobile users experiencing average jitter in medium density regions for biweekly periods from August 1, 2018, to December 14, 2018. The users are divided into excellent (0 to 4 ms), good (4 to 10 ms), adequate (10 to 20 ms), and poor (20+ ms) QoS levels.

Biweekly period	0 to 4 millisecs	4 to 10 millisecs	10 to 20 millisecs	20+ millisecs
Aug 1 - Aug 14	32.75%	52.49%	11.70%	3.06%
Sept 1 - Sept 14	36.70%	51.02%	10.07%	2.21%
Oct 1 - Oct 14	46.60%	45.37%	6.70%	1.33%
Nov 1 - Nov 14	45.13%	46.74%	6.78%	1.35%
Dec 1 - Dec 14	46.09%	45.83%	6.73%	1.35%
Average	41.45%	48.29%	8.39%	1.86%
Median	45.13%	46.74%	6.78%	1.35%
Standard deviation	6.32%	3.24%	2.34%	0.77%

Table 5.19: Percentage of mobile users experiencing average jitter in low density regions for biweekly periods from August 1, 2018, to December 14, 2018. The users are divided into excellent (0 to 4 ms), good (4 to 10 ms), adequate (10 to 20 ms), and poor (20+ ms) QoS levels.

5.3.1.5   Signal Strength

Figure 5.20 shows histograms representing signal strength of users in high, medium, and low density regions. The histograms have a bin size of 5 dBm. As the user count is variable for each density region within each biweekly period, the histograms have a normalized bin count. The number of users in each bin was normalized by the total number of users present in each density region for each biweekly period. Signal strength of users was analyzed by dividing the users into four different QoS levels such as excellent (-60+ dBm), good (-80 to -60 dBm), adequate (-100 to -80 dBm), and poor (-140 to -100 dBm). Tables 5.20, 5.21, and 5.22 show percentage of users receiving different levels of signal strength in high, medium, and low density regions.

5.3.1.5.1   High Density   The histograms for the high density region (Figure 5.20) are unimodal and nearly symmetric with a peak near -90 to -85 dBm. This suggests that half of the users in the high density region receive adequate to excellent signal strength. The number of users receiving different levels of signal strength over biweekly periods is more variable for the high density region (Table 5.20) than for medium and low density regions (Tables 5.21 and 5.22).

5.3.1.5.2   Medium Density   The average number of users receiving different levels of signal strength for the medium density region (Table 5.21) is very similar to the high density region (Table 5.20). Also, similar to the high density region, the histograms for the medium density region (Figure 5.20) are unimodal and nearly symmetric with a peak near -90 to -85 dBm. This suggests that users in the medium and high density regions receive similar signal strength over a sequence of biweekly periods.

5.3.1.5.3   Low Density   Unlike high and medium density regions, the histograms for the low density region are right-skewed with a peak around -100 to -95 dBm (Figure 5.20). This suggests that fewer users in the low density region receive good to excellent signal strength (-80 to -60+ dBm) as compared to high and medium density regions. This is also confirmed by Table 5.22, where more users receive poor signal strength (-140 to -100 dBm) in the low density region than in medium and high density regions (Tables 5.20 and 5.21). Furthermore, the histograms in the low density region (Figure 5.20) are consistent throughout each biweekly period suggesting that different levels of signal strength experienced by the users remains steady.

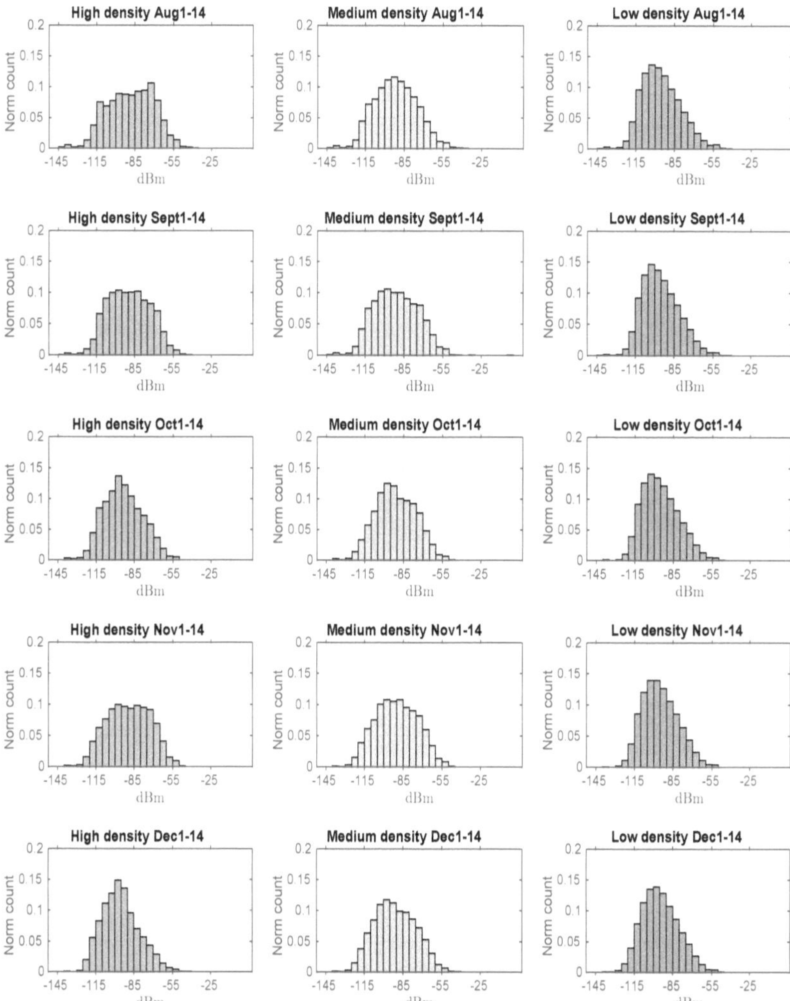

Figure 5.20: Histograms representing signal strength of mobile users in high, medium, and low density regions for biweekly periods between August 1, 2018, and December 14, 2018.

Biweekly period	-140 to -100 dBm	-100 to -80 dBm	-80 to -60 dBm	-60+ dBm
Aug 1 - Aug 14	28.06%	35.54%	32.34%	3.93%
Sept 1 - Sept 14	29.50%	40.43%	27.63%	2.40%
Oct 1 - Oct 14	35.73%	44.52%	18.55%	1.18%
Nov 1 - Nov 14	29.18%	38.61%	29.55%	2.66%
Dec 1 - Dec 14	39.78%	45.02%	14.12%	1.09%
Average	32.45%	40.82%	24.44%	2.25%
Median	29.50%	40.43%	27.63%	2.40%
Standard deviation	5.08%	4.01%	7.74%	1.17%

Table 5.20: Percentage of mobile users experiencing signal strength in high density regions for biweekly periods from August 1, 2018, to December 14, 2018. The users are divided into excellent (-60+ dBm), good (-80 to -60 dBm), adequate (-100 to -80 dBm), and poor (-140 to -100 dBm) QoS levels.

Biweekly period	-140 to -100 dBm	-100 to -80 dBm	-80 to -60 dBm	-60+ dBm
Aug 1 - Aug 14	31.68%	43.58%	22.18%	2.48%
Sept 1 - Sept 14	32.72%	39.62%	25.02%	2.57%
Oct 1 - Oct 14	29.91%	44.18%	24.26%	1.65%
Nov 1 - Nov 14	29.59%	41.48%	26.59%	2.34%
Dec 1 - Dec 14	31.38%	42.54%	24.07%	2.01%
Average	31.05%	42.28%	24.43%	2.21%
Median	31.38%	42.54%	24.26%	2.34%
Standard deviation	1.30%	1.81%	1.60%	0.38%

Table 5.21: Percentage of mobile users experiencing signal strength in medium density regions for biweekly periods from August 1, 2018, to December 14, 2018. The users are divided into excellent (-60+ dBm), good (-80 to -60 dBm), adequate (-100 to -80 dBm), and poor (-140 to -100 dBm) QoS levels.

Biweekly period	-140 to -100 dBm	-100 to -80 dBm	-80 to -60 dBm	-60+ dBm
Aug 1 - Aug 14	41.73%	42.78%	14.05%	1.37%
Sept 1 - Sept 14	41.78%	43.59%	13.56%	1.03%
Oct 1 - Oct 14	40.92%	43.71%	14.32%	1.04%
Nov 1 - Nov 14	39.45%	45.51%	14.17%	0.87%
Dec 1 - Dec 14	38.33%	46.00%	14.82%	0.86%
Average	40.44%	44.32%	14.18%	1.03%
Median	40.92%	43.71%	14.17%	1.03%
Standard deviation	1.51%	1.37%	0.45%	0.21%

Table 5.22: Percentage of mobile users experiencing signal strength in low density regions for biweekly periods from August 1, 2018, to December 14, 2018. The users are divided into excellent (-60+ dBm), good (-80 to -60 dBm), adequate (-100 to -80 dBm), and poor (-140 to -100 dBm) QoS levels.

5.3.1.6   Insights from QoS Analysis

Analyzing QoS parameters shows that users in the high and medium density regions receive better signal strength than users in the low density region. Based on the assumption that Manhattan Island has a uniform distribution of cellular towers, this suggests that users in the high and medium density regions are physically closer to the cellular towers than users in the low density region. The AD test results show that user density distribution is non-stationary over time; however, it is observed that the geographic locations related to high and medium density regions change over time, whereas the low density region remains similar. It is also observed that the QoS levels of low density regions are less variable as compared to medium and high density regions. Additionally, users from different density regions experience each QoS parameter differently in the mobile network. For example, users in the low density region experience higher download throughputs and lower jitter, whereas users in the medium density region experience higher upload throughputs and lower latencies. But overall, the users in the high density regions have lower QoS levels than medium and low density regions. As users have a higher likelihood of using mobile services in the high and medium density regions, it is beneficial for the mobile carriers to provide them with a better quality of service to prevent customer churn and increase profits.

5.4   Chapter Summary

Statistical analysis of the user density $\hat{p}(x)$ estimates was conducted using the Anderson Darling test to determine if the densities were stationary over the biweekly periods. The AD test was performed on a pair of subsequent biweekly periods to determine if the user density distributions varied over time. Due to large volume, the biweekly periods from October 15th onward were tested in shards to first determine the statistical similarity between the shards within the same period and then to determine similarities across periods. Based on the results, it was concluded that the user density distribution from one biweekly period was significantly different from the next biweekly period. Further analysis of the data was conducted by partitioning the data into three distinct user densities: high, medium, and low. The data was partitioned based on the top 33% and bottom 33% of the $\hat{p}(x)$ threshold values. Quality of Service of users from high, medium, and low densities was then compared using the following parameters: upload throughput, download throughput, average jitter, average latency, and signal strength. The results showed that the users in the high and medium density regions received better signal strength. However, users in the high density region got worse QoS than medium and low density regions. Also, the users' QoS levels for each biweekly period were more variable in the high density region than the medium and low density regions.

Chapter 6

Conclusions

This **book** analyzed the end-user quality of service in a mobile network using device-side measurements. User's satisfaction level with the network carrier is highly influenced by their perception of QoS. Providing satisfactory service to customers is one of the key objectives of a telecommunications company as poor-perceived QoS is one of the significant sources of customer churn. The goal of this **book** was to statistically analyze variability in user densities over time and its impact on user QoS in a wireless network. User densities were estimated by Kernel Density Estima-tion and Expectation Maximization. The k-sample Anderson Darling was then used to determine statistical stationarity of user densities over biweekly periods of data. Furthermore, for each biweekly period, the user densities were partitioned into high, medium, and low density areas. The users' QoS levels within these areas were then statisitically analyzed.

6.1   Results

The k-sample Anderson-Darling test was performed on data shards for biweekly periods with large volumes. The results showed that the data shards were statistically similar and came from a common user density distribution. The exception was for biweekly period November 1-14. Further AD testing showed that majority of data shards, i.e., 2 out of 3 shards have a similar user density distribution. The AD test was then performed on subsequent pairs of biweekly periods. The first data shard was chosen as the representative shard for periods containing shards. The results showed that the user density distributions were non-stationary from one biweekly period to the next.

Comparison of users' QoS levels between different areas of densities such as high, medium, and low showed that users in high density areas experienced lower QoS levels than those in medium and low density areas. Visual comparison of biweekly periods with high, medium, and low density areas showed that the high and medium density regions varied over time but the low density regions remained consistent. Also, users in high and medium density areas received a stronger network signal than in low density areas. This indicates that even though both high and medium density regions are dynamic, the users' QoS levels in high density regions are adversely affected than medium density regions.

6.2 Further Analyses

This book assessed the impact of user densities on quality of service by examining data from biweekly periods for a duration of five months. As observed, user densities are highly dynamic in urban areas. Therefore, long-term statistical analyses of user densities are needed for better network planning and placement of cellular towers and wireless access points. Currently, the book assesses different density regions over time; however, these regions change geographically. Also, the distribution of cellular towers of different geographical yet similar density regions is not known. Further statistical analyses can be supplemented with cellular tower information which can then be used to understand the variability of QoS levels of high density regions over time.

Appendix A

Additional Information

A.1   Great Circle Distance Query

Below is an example of an SQL query used to retrieve data. The query retrieves data within a twenty-five mile radius of Manhattan coordinates, 40.7831 latitude and -73.9712 longitude. Data was retrieved with QoS_Date ranging from August 01, 2018, to August 14, 2018.

```sql
CREATE TEMP FUNCTION RADIANS(x FLOAT64) AS (
  ACOS(-1) * x / 180
);
SELECT *
FROM
(
SELECT * ,
  (
  3959 * acos (
  cos (RADIANS(40.7831) )
  * cos( RADIANS( Location_Latitude ) )
  * cos( RADIANS( Location_Longitude ) - RADIANS(-73.9712) )
  + sin ( RADIANS(40.7831) )
  * sin ( RADIANS( Location_Latitude ) )
  )
  ) AS distance
FROM Standard_US.UnitedStates_MobileOnly_20180801to20181231
) as innerTable
Where distance < 25
AND
QOS_DATE between
"2018-08-01 00:00:00 UTC" AND "2018-08-14 23:59:00 UTC"
```

A.2 Estimated PDF of Mobile Network Data

The following plots depict estimated user density PDFs, $\hat{p}(\boldsymbol{x})$, for each biweekly period. The figures' $\hat{p}(\boldsymbol{x})$ axes corresponds to the estimated probability for a given latitude and longitude. Also, the $\hat{p}(\boldsymbol{x})$ axes have an upper limit of 10^{-6} to help visualize high density regions such as in Figures A.5 and A.6. The grey regions in the plots represent $\hat{p}(\boldsymbol{x})$ values below $1.0 * 10^{-8}$.

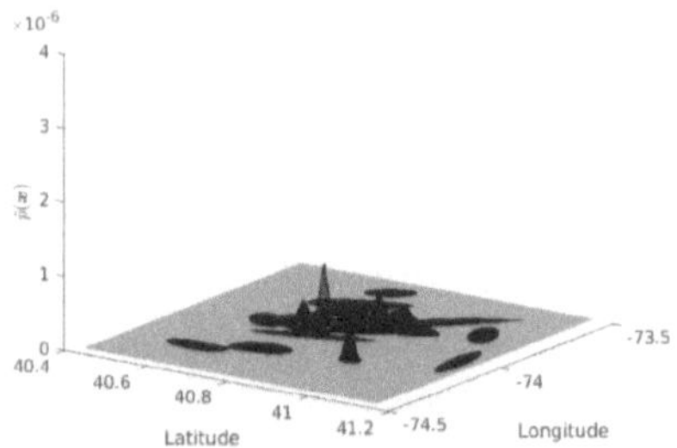

Figure A.1: $\hat{p}(\boldsymbol{x})$ for August 1-August 14, 2018.

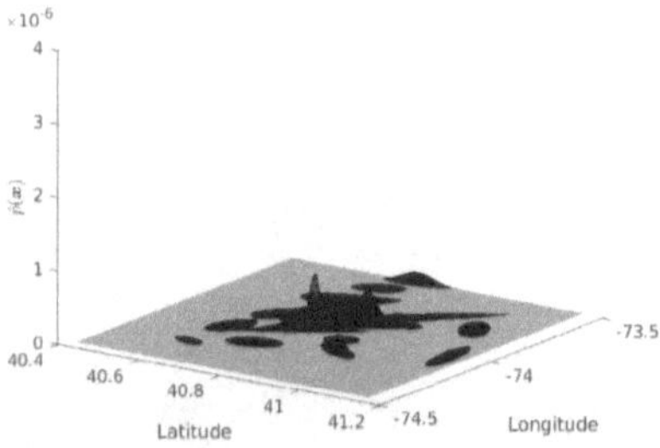

Figure A.2: $\hat{p}(\boldsymbol{x})$ for August 15-August 31, 2018.

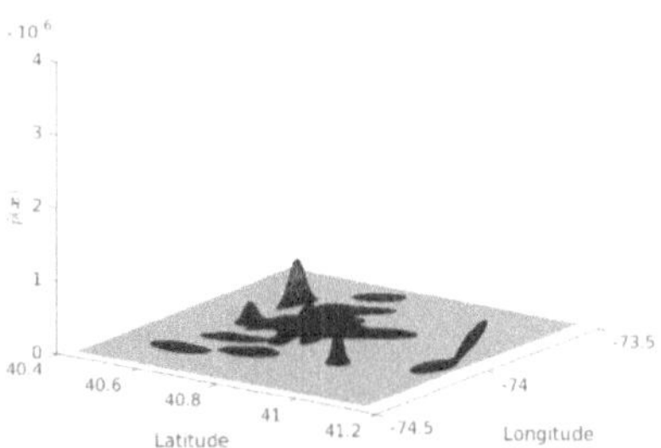

Figure A.3: $\hat{p}(\boldsymbol{x})$ for September 1-September 14, 2018.

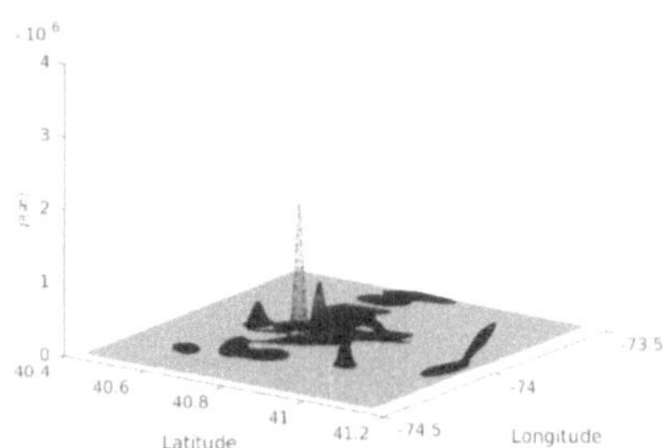

Figure A.4: $\hat{p}(\boldsymbol{x})$ for September 15-September 30, 2018.

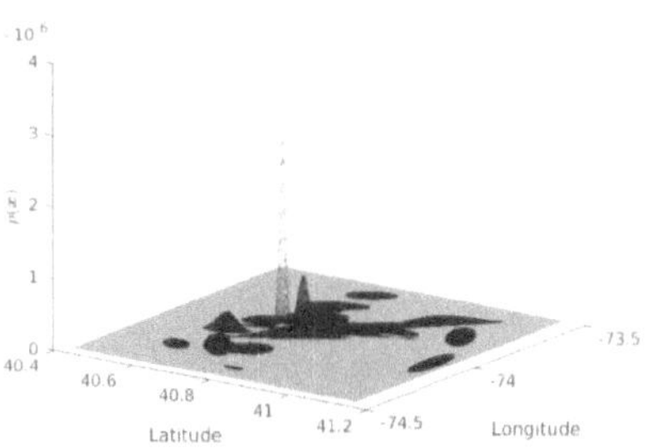

Figure A.5: $\hat{p}(\boldsymbol{x})$ for October 1-October 14, 2018.

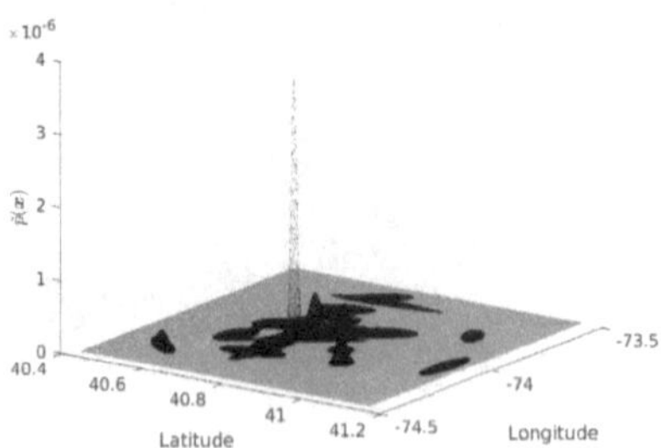

(a) $\hat{p}(\boldsymbol{x})$ for October 15-October 31 for data Shard no. 1.

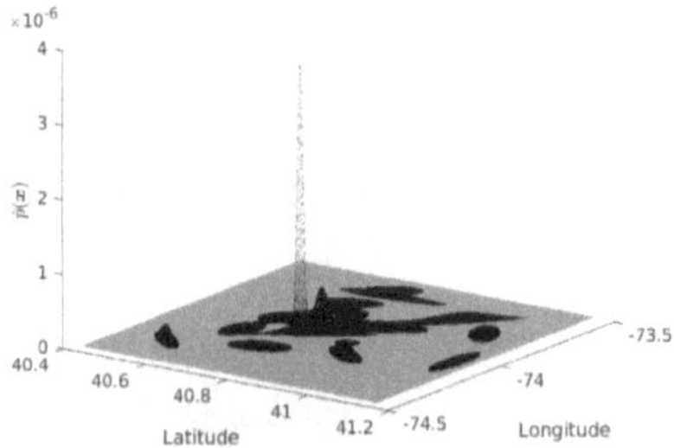

(b) $\hat{p}(\boldsymbol{x})$ for October 15-October 31 for data Shard no. 2.

Figure A.6: $\hat{p}(\boldsymbol{x})$ for October 15-October 31, 2018.

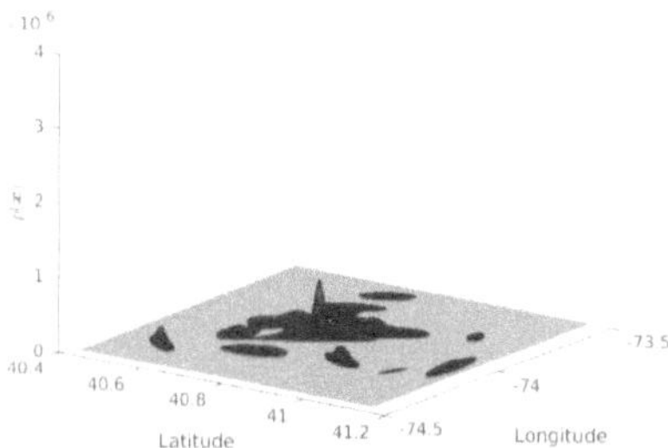

(a) $\hat{p}(\boldsymbol{x})$ for November 1-November 14 for data Shard no. 1.

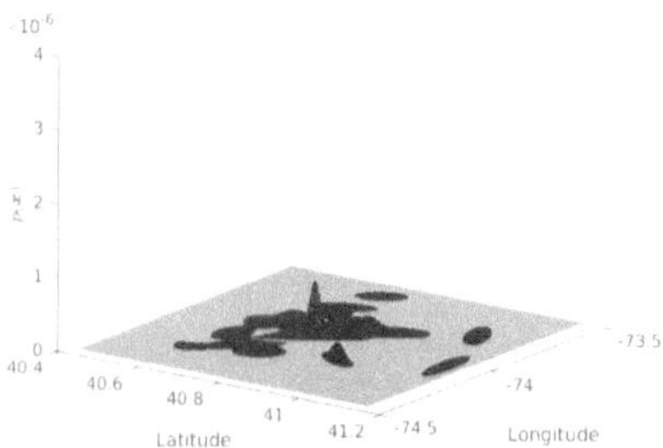

(b) $\hat{p}(\boldsymbol{x})$ for November 1-November 14 for data Shard no. 2.

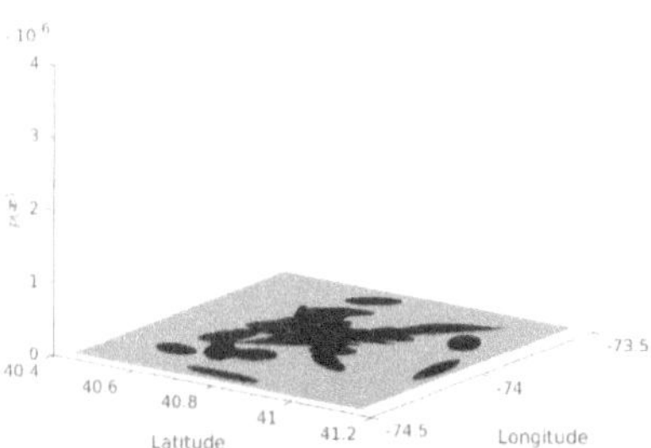

(c) $\hat{p}(\boldsymbol{x})$ for November 1-November 14 for data Shard no. 3.

Figure A.7: $\hat{p}(\boldsymbol{x})$ for November 1-November 14, 2018.

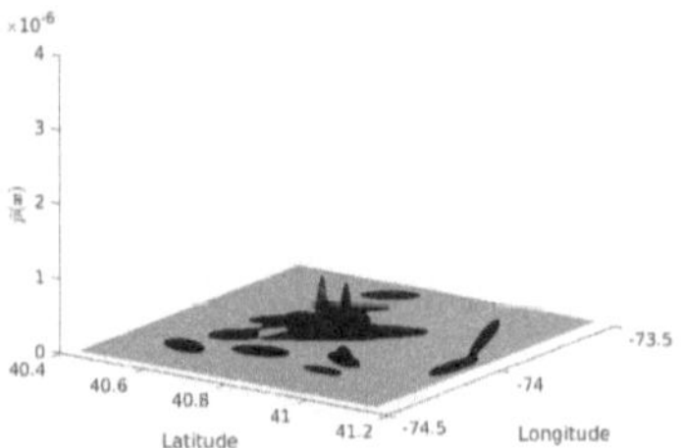

(a) $\hat{p}(\boldsymbol{x})$ for November 15-November 30 for data Shard no. 1.

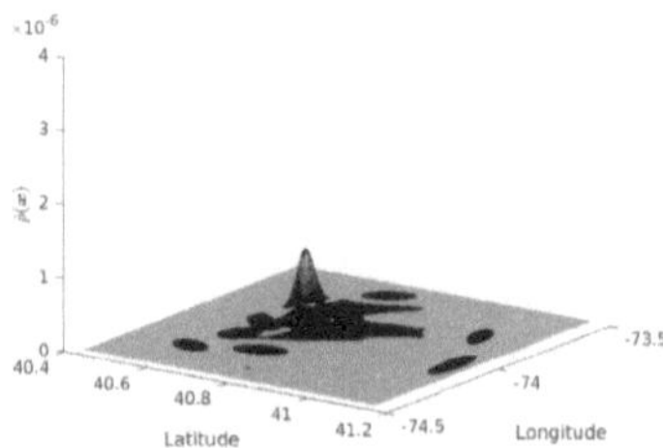

(b) $\hat{p}(\boldsymbol{x})$ for November 15-November 30 for data Shard no. 2.

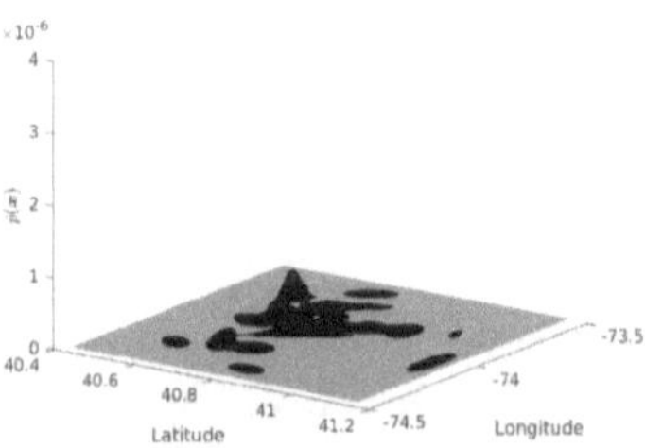

(c) $\hat{p}(\boldsymbol{x})$ for November 15-November 30 for data Shard no. 3.

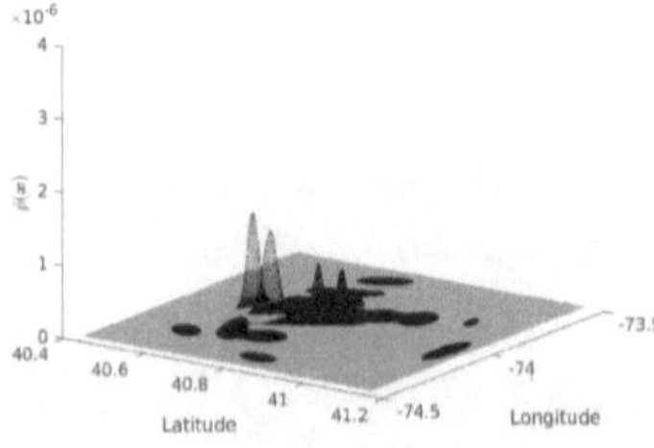

(d) $\hat{p}(\boldsymbol{x})$ for November 15-November 30 for data Shard no. 4.

Figure A.8: $\hat{p}(\boldsymbol{x})$ for November 15-November 30, 2018.

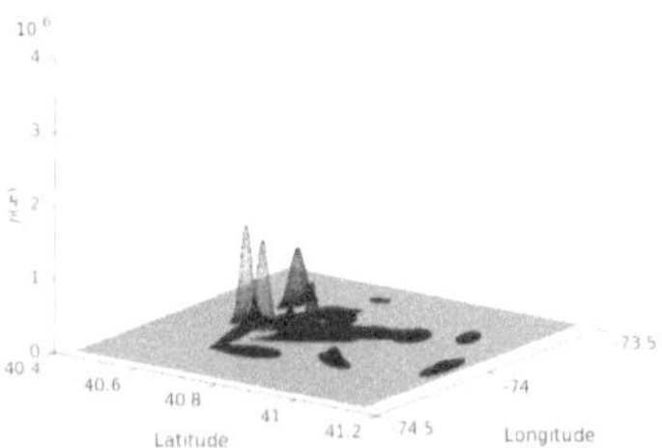

(a) $\hat{p}(\boldsymbol{x})$ for December 1-December 14 for data Shard no. 1.

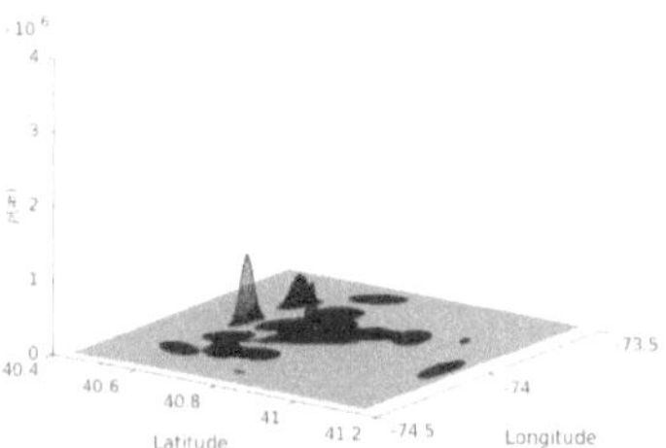

(b) $\hat{p}(\boldsymbol{x})$ for December 1-December 14 for data Shard no. 2.

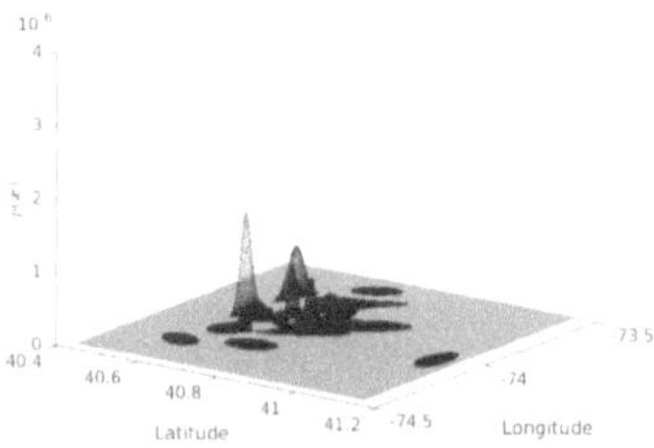

(c) $\hat{p}(\boldsymbol{x})$ for December 1-December 14 for data Shard no. 3.

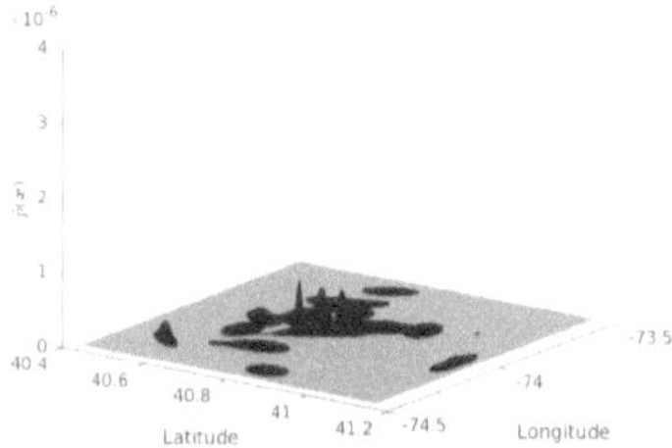

(d) $\hat{p}(\boldsymbol{x})$ for December 1-December 14 for data Shard no. 4.

Figure A.9: $\hat{p}(\boldsymbol{x})$ for December 1-December 14, 2018.

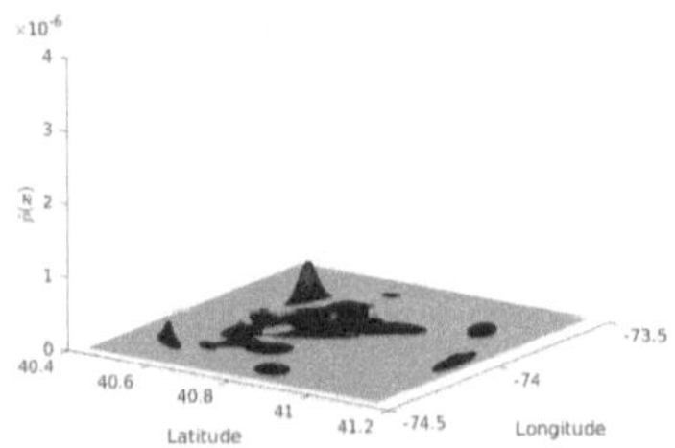

(a) $\hat{p}(\boldsymbol{x})$ for December 15-December 31 for data Shard no. 1.

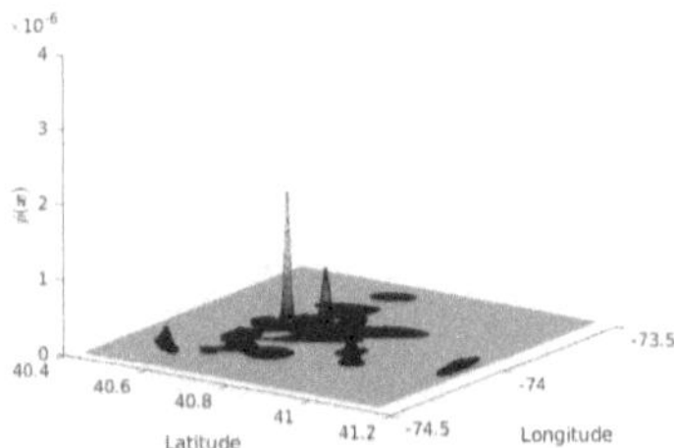

(b) $\hat{p}(\boldsymbol{x})$ for December 15-December 31 for data Shard no. 2.

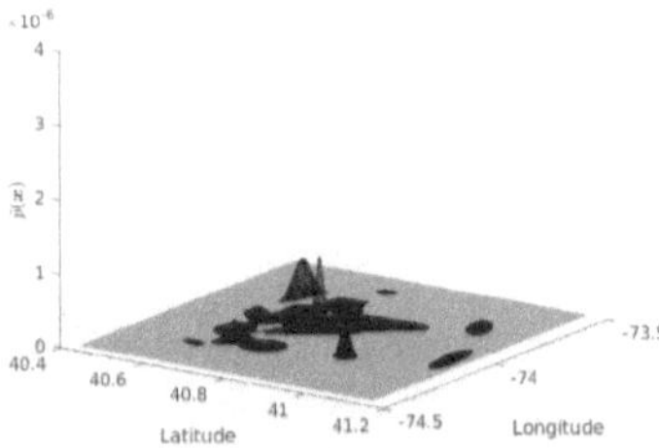

(c) $\hat{p}(\boldsymbol{x})$ for December 15-December 31 for data Shard no. 3.

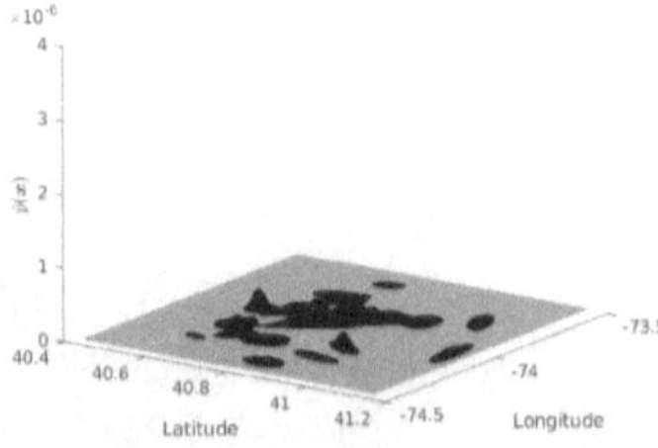

(d) $\hat{p}(\boldsymbol{x})$ for December 15-December 31 for data Shard no. 4.

Figure A.10: $\hat{p}(\boldsymbol{x})$ for December 15-December 31, 2018.